Iron-Man Christianity

THE ONLY WINNING STRATEGY:
"Follow Me."
There is no Plan B.

WALLACE FRANCIS
with ED ELLIS

D1457228

LifeSource Essentials Ministries, Inc.
Cumming, Georgia 30041

Published by LifeSource Creations
www.lifesourcecreations.com

Book Layout ©2013 BookDesignTemplates.com

Ordering Information:
Quantity sales. Special discounts are available on quantity purchases by corporations, associations, and others. For details, contact the "Special Sales Department" at the address in the Appendix section or email at <www.wfimc89@yahoo.com>.

IRON-MAN CHRISTIANITY / Wallace Francis & Ed Ellis
ISBN: 978-0-9908762-0-5

This book is dedicated to

Joseph Carroll

And the staff of the Evangelical Institute who preached
Christ, practiced the way of the cross, and had an eternal impact
on me and my family. I learned through them that Christianity
is a Person, Jesus Christ Himself.

Worship Him, walk with Him, witness unto Him.

"*Iron-Man Christianity* is the perfect call for any team. It is the perfect blend of the toughness of the game of football and love. Many coaches would not use those two words together: Football and Love. But Vince Lombardi knew what it would take to build championship teams. Taking people from all walks of life and blending them together using the Biblical principles that Christ used to build His foundation in the church. Wallace Francis, in *Iron-Man Christianity,* has captured the perfect walk for any athlete or team."

June Jones
Former Atlanta Falcons Head Coach

TABLE OF CONTENTS

Section One

Section Two

ACKNOWLEDGEMENTS

The authors would like to give a special thanks to two authors whose works allowed great insight into a great man, Vince Lombardi. First, thanks to all-pro guard Jerry Kramer. His intense and heartfelt appreciation for Lombardi, what he stood for, and his life-changing impact on so many of the players who played for him is amply testified to in his bio-books on Lombardi. Especially helpful was his book, *Lombardi: Winning is the Only Thing*, where he allows dozens of former players and coaches to recount Lombardi's impact on their lives. It is a tremendous legacy. One thing is for sure, if Lombardi were still alive, he would not rest (nor allow anyone else to rest!) until Jerry Kramer's name was added to the NFL Hall of Fame.

The other acknowledgment is to John Eisenberg for his book *That First Season,* where he recounts in vivid detail how Lombardi approached the task of turning losers into winners in Green Bay that first year. He brought it to life like no other book I have ever read. It is a great story.

Finally, we owe an enormous debt of gratitude to the many reviewers who offered timely insights, comments, and corrections along the way, and helped make this book what it is. To Travis, Art, Doug, Dixon, Bobby, Abigail, Jeff, Derry, and other laborers who gave hours to making this book a reality, we could not have done it without you. We thank the Lord for you.

INTRODUCTION

We want to be clear from the beginning. This book has nothing to do with comic book characters or triathlons. It is about who will win what the apostle Paul calls "the crown of life."

The title of this book, *Iron-Man Christianity*, is drawn from what was once known as single-platoon football. Most of us have forgotten (or were too young to know) that it was not until the early 1960's that NCAA college and professional football rules permanently allowed unlimited player substitutions during any play in the game. Why is that important? Because it completely changed the game.

Prior to this (except for the WWII era) only limited substitutions were allowed and this resulted in most players having to play both offense and defense! Needless to say, that idea is really unthinkable today, but back then it was the norm. It was expected that most players had to learn the skills necessary to play one offensive position and one defensive position.

Winning under those conditions is going to require dedication, discipline, and commitment—from the whole team. The players had to fulfill their roles on both offense and defense. In the early days of football, it was not unusual at all. It was expected. They had a name for this.

IT WAS CALLED *IRON-MAN* FOOTBALL.

The reality is that true Christianity is more akin to what was once called "Iron-Man football." Vince Lombardi was an Iron-

Man—and he built the Packers into an Iron-Man football team. They just did not know it at the beginning.

FOREWORD

No one could remember seeing so many professional athletes puking on the sidelines, certainly not in Green Bay, Wisconsin.

In 1959, after the first week of practice for the new football season, a lot of Green Bay Packers were thinking about looking for jobs in other places! Vince Lombardi knew there would be a price to pay for success. This was his first year. He did not know how many games they could win in 1959, but he was determined they would not lose because they were not in top shape! He was also determined that everyone they played would know one thing—the Packers would be tough to beat! Every week!

It has been over 50 years since that football dynasty ended and many have forgotten or never knew how it first came into being; how an unknown, first-time head coach turned the most unlikely group of losers into a football dynasty.

Vince Lombardi took 22 men and turned them into a legendary football dynasty that dominated the National Football League for nine years. That was (and still is) considered an amazing accomplishment. But it doesn't begin to compare to the accomplishment of Jesus Christ. He took just 12 men and changed the world—forever!

The parallels to the leadership styles of both men reveal the keys to success, in sports and in life. We will look at a number of them in this book. But the fundamental key to success for both men was actually very simple. They knew how to win. They also knew what it would take to win. All they needed to know from the players was the answer to this question:

WILL YOU FOLLOW ME?

For the Christian (or those considering their next step), the instructions are clear. To paraphrase Jesus Christ,

IF YOU WANT TO WIN, YOU MUST FOLLOW ME; THERE IS NO PLAN B.

What does that mean? What does it mean to follow Jesus Christ? This is what we want to learn. It is the key to Christianity.

This is a story of what it means to follow and the rewards you can reap when you do it right.

Wallace Francis

Iron-Man
Christianity

Chapter One

The Story of "Titletown, USA"

"The Packers hired who?"

That was the question reverberating all over Green Bay, Wisconsin, the afternoon of January 28, 1959. Nobody in the small town of Green Bay, had ever heard of Vince Lombardi. Even most of the players had not heard of him. But he was the person the forty-six-man Executive Committee (which ran the Green Bay Packer organization) had just chosen to be the new head coach of their struggling football team.

What was even more stunning was that he was being designated both the Head Coach and the General Manager—and he was also not going to have to report every week to the Executive Committee. Lombardi was being given total control of the team: the hires, the fires, who to draft and who to trade. For better or worse, this was going to be his team. This was a major departure from the way things had always run in Green Bay, but the owners were desperate to turn the franchise into a winner. It was a new day in Packer town; everyone seemed either shocked or fearful, that is, everyone except Vince Lombardi. He was excited. He was excited to be a head coach in the NFL, but he didn't have much to be excited about when he considered the current Packer team.

The Enigma of the Packers: Hall of Fame Losers

An enigma is an undeniable fact or truth that makes no sense; it is a mystery, a confusing puzzle.

The fact is simple. In 1958, the Green Bay Packers were losers. They were coming off a 1-10-1 season. You have to be really bad to lose that many games at the professional level.

The puzzling enigma is that their roster reads like a "Who's Who" of NFL Hall of Fame royalty! To anyone in the Baby Boomer generation, these names are household names. Listen to it: Bart Starr, Paul Hornung, Jerry Kramer, Jim Taylor, Max McGee, Ray Nitschke, Don McIlhenny, Forrest Gregg, Babe Parilli, Jim Ringo; they are all famous now. Most of them are in the NFL Hall of Fame.

But in 1958 they were just a bunch of losers—with a record of 1-10-1. What changed? What turned this bunch of losers into winners? How did Green Bay ultimately become known as "Titletown, USA"? One man made the difference. His name: Vince Lombardi. He is a legend now, but his arrival in Green Bay that cold winter day was a rude awakening for many in the beginning. How did he engineer such a magical turnaround so quickly?

A New Day in Green Bay

When Lombardi first arrived in Green Bay in January 1959, nobody knew who he was. Assistant coaches were not commonly known by fans or players. The fact that he had been on winning New York Giants teams was lost on the Packer faithful. As far as they were concerned, he was unknown and unproven. The Packers desperately needed a winner. Lombardi was a huge risk.

Lombardi knew all this. He knew there was no reason for the fans to believe in him. He had no name, no established reputation that would immediately command respect from the players. What could he say? What would he do to instill some confidence in his ability? The answer was pretty simple: Do what he was hired to do: coach the team.

His biggest challenge was clear. How was he going to convince his players that if they would follow him, He would make them winners?

The only thing he had to begin with was his authority as coach. He was the Head Coach now; they had to respect that. Lombardi had to make sure they did. He had to assume that authority. Even more important, Lombardi had to convince them to follow him. They had to believe that he could make them winners.

Important Point:

Following is not the same as faith; at least not committed, saving faith. In fact, in the Scriptures, it is often seen as the first step toward that committed, saving faith. Jesus often encouraged it.

We fully agree with the biblical teaching that those who put their trust in Christ for salvation will follow Him (John 10:27-28). But there is also a very biblical (and often overlooked) concept of following that precedes and leads to that saving faith, and much of our modern-day efforts to evangelize the lost ignores this. What do we mean?

In our efforts to evangelize we are often sharing the gospel with people who do not know they are lost and do not realize they need a Savior. They hear gospel truth, give intellectual assent to its facts, but nothing in their life changes. Why? To put it in a familiar metaphor, it would be like a farmer expecting a crop by spreading seed on ground which had not been plowed up first. He would know it would be a dismal failure. The ground would still be hard and rocky, full of weeds and thorns; and there would be no place for the seed to take root.

This is what is happening to much of our evangelistic efforts today. Nobody wants to do the dirty work of plowing the soil so it is ready to receive the "seed" of the gospel. No one wants to make anyone feel uncomfortable by telling them where the consequences of sin and rebellion against a holy God will lead. You are not being their judge, you have absolutely no authority to judge. All judgment has been given to Jesus Christ by His Father. You are simply sharing what God has determined and declared is a violation of His law and results in judgment.

This is the dirty work that creates the need for the Savior which the gospel offers. Telling people about the salvation which comes through faith in Jesus Christ is *not* the dirty work. The gospel is only good news to a person who realizes he is lost and doomed!

We believe it makes a lot more sense to ask people to consider following Christ in a way that allows them to learn more about the truth of the gospel, about heaven and hell, the real truth about God, themselves, and the love of Christ. Then, having learned enough, they can make an intelligent life decision as to whether they want to follow Him as Lord and Savior or choose not to.

It was a Common New Testament Experience

If you read through the New Testament, you will find that multitudes followed Jesus for a time, learned about His teachings, experienced some of His healings and miracles, and then made the decision to trust Him and follow Him—or turn back. And Jesus honored their decisions.

If we need a biblical example of this approach, we need only look at what the Lord Himself did in the first chapter of John's gospel. Two of John the Baptist's disciples heard him say, "Behold, the Lamb of God." This got their attention! They wanted to learn more. So what did they do? They followed Jesus. The Lord realized they were following Him and turned and said to them, "What do you seek?" They asked where He was staying. They wanted to know how they could learn more about Him. What was His response? "Come and you will see." That is the point.

Our job is to encourage people to "come and see," find out enough about the truth of the gospel to see whether they need a Savior and want to put their trust in Him for the salvation which He offers. We know that only the Holy Spirit can save a soul. Our job is to reveal the need and point them to Christ, God's solution to their personal need.

Following is being willing to learn, being willing to give the leader a chance to teach you what he wants you to know. Out of that knowledge and experience you should have a solid, rational basis for true faith. That kind of following will lead either to a committed, wholehearted, and well-grounded faith, or a decision to turn away. Anything less will collapse under the inevitable pressures it will face in life. Lombardi understood this principle.

Jesus could do miracles to validate His teaching and draw multitudes to hear Him. Vince Lombardi could not do that, but he did have one big advantage to start with: the Packers were "hired hands." If they wanted to be able to cash their paychecks, they had to come and at least give Lombardi a chance. It is often said, "Agony comes before the ecstasy." I guess this idea is most familiar to mothers who have gone through the labor pains of giving birth, then get to enjoy the delight of holding their newborn child. But during those first days in the Packer's training camp, nobody could see the ecstasy; they were consumed with the agony. They thought a lunatic was running the team! And this was just the beginning of the Iron-Man era in Green Bay.

That First Lombardi Training Camp

Historically, summer training camps for the Packers were more like mini-vacations than real workouts. This was the team culture Lombardi inherited when he arrived. But he knew that could not continue if this team was ever to win again. Toughness was at the core of Lombardi's strategy. Winning would require dedication and discipline, neither of which the current Packer team seemed to have much of. Lombardi was about to find out who had it and who did not.

Lombardi believed in toughness: Fourth quarter toughness. That meant you had to be in top physical shape. In most pre-season training camps, some players are required to report in before others to get oriented to any new changes in the offense or defense. This meant they would be the first ones to experience what training camp will be like that year. That year the experience was shocking!

Players who were there were calling their buddies who had not reported yet and telling them that Lombardi was insane! They had not seen so many guys puking on the sidelines in their entire NFL careers. Lombardi also set curfews, strict diets, tightly scheduled practices, and team meetings early in the mornings so there would be no question that all their time would be consumed with football. Lombardi simply took complete charge of their lives.

This discipline was going to be essential because he intended to make enormous changes, in both personnel and playing strategy. There would be a new offense, a new defense, and players playing new positions. But it had to be done if he was going to turn these losers into winners and this team into a title contender.

The Lesson to Learn

The lesson to learn here is about leaders and followers. Lombardi became an outstanding leader because for many years he was an outstanding follower. When he coached for "Red" Blaik at Army, he embraced and absorbed all he could learn from the Army head coach: his strategy, his discipline, and his simplicity. You can mark it down: somewhere along the line a good leader learned to be a good leader by being a good follower first.

The same lesson is true for Christians. It was true for the Lord Himself. It was true that Jesus Christ was God, so one would assume He needed no instruction, no guidance, and no one to answer to. But that was not the case.

His whole life was lived in submission to His Father. He learned from His Father and He lived in His Presence constantly. He said that He never decided on His own what the next "play" was going to be in His life. He lived to do His Father's will. His goal in life was to glorify the Father. Nothing else.

At every point and in every way, He followed His Father's leading. This meant living in submission to His parents until He was thirty years old. He lived as a carpenter's helper and spent His free time learning the Hebrew Scriptures. He was a brilliant student and had more wisdom and understanding than His teachers. Yet He never became proud, arrogant, or over-confident. He continued to be a humble follower of God.

But as the Scriptures describe it, when His hour had come, He did not hesitate to begin to share the truth of the gospel, calling men to repentance and faith and to "Follow Me."

The Application to Us

If we are to be useful to the Lord, we must be His true followers. If we are going to lead, we must first learn to follow. We are no different from the Packers. We all start out losers. Our past record is abysmal, sufficient to send us to hell forever. But none of the past matters. Please do not gloss over this! None of the past matters now. It did not matter to Lombardi, and it did not matter to the Lord when He called His disciples to follow Him. The only thing that matters is how we respond to His call now.

That is the only issue in any life. What will you say to His call to "follow" Him **now**?

Are we willing to follow Him? Are we willing to learn from Him and see if what He is saying is the real truth? If we are willing, He will teach us what we need to know. He will teach us what the real goal in our life should be, what "plays" we need to be running. Even more, He will give us **all** the "gifts," **all** the abilities we need to accomplish His plan and His eternal purpose for our lives. If we are willing to follow Him, He will make us winners! And He will make us winners in the only game that really counts, the game of life.

So how did it turn out for the Packers that first season? Better than Lombardi expected.

Chapter Two

Is Winning Biblical?

Before we see how the Packers began their march into history, we need to address this issue right up front. Some folks today want to try to minimize the pain of losing by eliminating it. In a misguided attempt to protect the supposedly fragile egos of our young people from the damaging humiliation of losing, they are refusing to allow them to play games where one person wins and the other loses. Short of that, they prohibit teams from winning big, i.e., stronger teams running up the score on weaker teams. Examples are endless. Here is why I believe this makes no sense.

In the course of my life, I have played football, basketball, baseball, and now, golf (sort of). The listing there is instructive. As my body has continued to break down over the years, I have had to resort to games in which I could still function and compete. While I have enjoyed much success in winning, there is no doubt that I have lost more than I have won. That is really important! Why? It made me better!

The reason is simple. I always wanted to play with people who were better than I was. I am very grateful they were willing to play with me. But it also meant that I lost more than I won. Why would I do this? The answer is so simple! I did it because I wanted to get better! I wanted to achieve more. Everyone wants to win, but today many never have the chance to learn *how* to win.

You cannot learn much from people who are not better than you are. The better the competition, the more you will be challenged. That is the point. But make no mistake about it, I always wanted to win and I played to win. I believed that, eventually, I would win. But losing was necessary to that process.

Winning and Losing Are Part of Life

You do not have to go very far into the animal kingdom to realize that winning and losing are part of life. When the lion and the tiger face off, one is going to win and the other will lose, and losing will likely cost them their life. This is simply the world we live in. Fortunately, most of our modern daily human battles are not matters of life and death.

Battles in life are unavoidable. In a world full of sinful men and women and a cursed creation, you are not going to see the lions lying down with the lambs, not for a while yet. You are going to see lots of tribulations, lots of adversity, and lots of selfishness which is going to lead to lots of battles. In those battles, you are going to see victory and defeat.

The real world of life does not believe much in games which end in a tie. So why are we training our kids as if it did?

The truth is winning is biblical. But somehow many of our well-meaning, politically correct contemporaries believe that if our kids do not experience the humbling that comes from losing, they will be stronger or at least less emotionally damaged. We wonder what part of the world people live in who come up with such fuzzy thinking. It certainly bears no resemblance to the world that most of us get up and face every day.

Of course, the reality is that many of the folks functioning in the elite academic world never actually engage with or live in the real world in which the rest of us live. This isolation creates a serious barrier to clear thinking about how to prepare our kids for those real world challenges they are going to face.

Too many in our generation have forgotten that one of the primary purposes of traditional education was the molding of character, as well as the training in basic life skills. It used to be a cooperative effort between parents and educators. Over the years, as the authority to discipline was removed from the educators, the task of education was reduced to merely communicating essential information. Words fail to describe the fiasco we now see in our modern public schools.

To be clear, we are in no way condoning those extreme situations where someone is being totally and unnecessarily humiliated. Some people are just mean-spirited (their day of reckoning will come). But for the most part, the challenges and adversity we face in life (even as young people) are what help to build our character. We see this all the time in sports. And this is biblical!

The apostle Paul put it like this:

> "And not only this, but we also exult in our tribulations, knowing that tribulation brings about perseverance; and perseverance, proven character; and proven character, hope."   —Romans 5:3-4

In the Bible, except for times of judgment, tribulation is presented as a positive. Tribulation is from an old Latin word which means "to press." It was used to describe what happened when grains were rubbed and pressed against a threshing board with sharp points. The idea is that what is left after the outer layers are rubbed off is good and useable. It is a similar idea to purifying precious metals by burning off the dross by melting the metal. What is left is pure and strong and can be used in productive ways.

So trials and tribulations are almost always good things, needful if the best "product" is to be produced. But does that translate to "winning"? Absolutely!

God says, "Run to Win"

The apostle Paul says it clearly in 1 Corinthians, chapter 9. Here he uses the word "win" six times in five verses, and the meaning is exactly what we mean when we use the word today. Paul uses the word in an athletic context to describe how life is to be lived. The Goal is to WIN!

> "Do you not know that those who run in a race all run,
> but only one receives the prize? Run in such a way that
> you may win." —1 Corinthians 9:24

When we emphasize the importance of running the race of life in a way that allows you to win, we are on solid biblical ground, regardless of what the current, cultural psycho-babble may be promoting. You either win or you lose in the race of life. There are no tie games or do-overs.

We believe that what the Bible says is truth; truth we can rely on. God's truth never, ever changes, period. The apostle Paul put it this way:

> "All Scripture is inspired by God (literally "God-

breathed") and profitable for teaching, for reproof, for correction, for training in righteousness; so that the man of God may be adequate, equipped for every good work."   —2 Timothy 3:16-17

The "good work" we want to prepare for is winning the race. The next question you have to ask yourself becomes critically important: *Who do you go to learn about winning?* The answer, of course, is, you go to winners.

We can learn a lot about winning from Vince Lombardi. No one disputes that he was a winner!

Chapter Three

That Winning Feeling

"Winners never quit, quitters never win."
—Vince Lombardi

There were times the Packer players must have wondered if Lombardi had been reading his Bible and gotten stuck when he read the phrase, "Be ye perfect." That was precisely what Lombardi seemed to expect out of these players, and they were right. That was exactly his goal! He made them run plays over and over and over, trying to do just one thing, get it perfect, no mistakes.

The practices were brutal. Quarterback Babe Parilli said the only thing to compare them to were the legendary training camps which famous Alabama Coach Paul "Bear" Bryant used to run. Most described his camps as more of a "survival" challenge than training camp. They eventually wrote a book and made a movie, *The Junction Boys,* about the 1954 summer training camp when he coached at Texas A&M. Like Bear Bryant, Lombardi's strategy seemed to be that if you could make it through the gauntlet of his training camp, then you might just have the dedication and discipline it was going to take to win in the NFL.

Did his strategy work? Well, the Packers did win the first three games of the new season, beating the Lions, the Bears and the San Francisco 49ers. And the folks in Green Bay began to wonder if Vince Lombardi might not actually be the Messiah in disguise. Packers' fans went nuts!

The taste of winning was intoxicating to the players. Many had almost forgotten what it was like. The memories of all the pain and suffering they had endured at training camp were fading. The players were beginning to see what Lombardi's strategy could produce. They were beginning to believe in him. They were winning. They saw the results. But they also learned another critical lesson.

Winning Does Not Mean Never Losing!

As of this writing, we are coming up to the 48th Super Bowl (Denver Broncos vs. Seattle Seahawks). They are the winners of the AFC and NFC championships, respectively. Both have had championship winning seasons, but both have also lost games. Losing a game does not mean you are not a winner. This is critically important to understand.

In the entire NFL history of Super Bowl champions, only one team has finished the season with a perfect record and also won the Super Bowl. The 1972 Miami Dolphins are the only team to have a perfect regular and post-season record. The New England Patriots almost did it in 2007. They went into the Super Bowl that year 18-0, but lost to the New York Giants. Were the Patriots losers? It is a silly question.

They lost the Super Bowl—and endured a great disappointment. But nobody thinks of that team as losers. It is very important to grasp this point.

Just because you lose a game does not mean you are a loser. The only way to truly become a loser is to quit. Once you quit, you give up the possibility of winning—and becoming a winner.

Adversity causes some men to break; others to break records.
—William Arthur Ward

The Green Bay Packers were about to face a huge challenge in their transformation into winners. After the euphoria of winning the first three games of the season, they lost the next five games! In a 12-game season, that is a lot of disappointment. But two of those games were to that year's NFL champion Baltimore Colts. Those were the golden years for the Colts; the years when the John Unitas-led teams included Lenny Moore and Raymond Berry. They also lost very tough games to the Bears and the Giants.

The good news was that they turned around and won the last four games of the season to end up with a winning 7-5 record. Lombardi was very proud of his team that year. Why? They missed the playoffs and barely had a winning record.

Lombardi was proud of his team because they did not quit! In the middle of the season, they hit a 5-game losing streak. They could easily have said to themselves, "This is not working!" They could have given up, given up on Lombardi, given up on the team, and given up on winning. But they did not quit. They overcame the adversity and became stronger.

There is a strong biblical exhortation that encourages us in the same way. In Galatians 6:9. Paul says:

> "Do not be deceived, God is not mocked; for whatever a
> man sows, this he will also reap.... Let us not lose heart

> in doing good, for in due time we will reap if we do not
> grow weary."   —Galatians 6:9

The Packers realized that even though they lost those games, they were **in** every game. No team had shut out the Packers that year. They had a chance to win almost every game. They knew they had made mistakes and they were the difference in those games. But they also knew those mistakes could be corrected. The Packers sensed they were no longer out-classed by other teams. Mentally, they began to believe they could win. And they believed Lombardi could lead them where they wanted to go. He could make them winners. Do we have this attitude in our Christian lives? Are we **in** every game? Are we in danger of losing heart? We have an encouragement that the Packers never had. We know the score at the end of the game. Christ wins in a shutout!

The Lessons for Us

The beginning is not the end–don't confuse them.
                                    —Wallace Francis

Too many committed Christian young men and women spend a lot of valuable time moaning over their failures and mistakes, some past, some present. This is a waste of time. This is not to minimize acts of sin in any way. But God knows there will be failures on the path of life. The enemy has plenty of distractions and temptations he will use to try to deceive us into making wrong decisions. He is a master at crafting temptations so that they are particularly attractive to you, and at times when you are most vulnerable. The key is to recognize them immediately, confess the sin, and get back onto the path.

Lombardi did not care about a player's past performance. He only cared about now. What are you going to give me now? The same is true of a Christian. When you turned from your old, selfish life and placed your faith and trust in Christ, you were "born again of the Spirit." This means many things, but one of the most important things it means is that your sinful past is now wiped out; it is deleted from God's memory bank, it is gone forever, period. (See Jeremiah 31:34 if you doubt this.)

What does this mean? It means just what it says. The day you are born again is the first day of your new life in Christ. It means you begin this life with No Past, No History, No Record of Failures. It is a clean start, a divine "do-over," only this time your eternal destiny is already decided. And it is good! My spiritual mentor, Joseph Carroll, used to put it this way:

"Christianity is a life of multiplied new beginnings."

That is a great truth to remember always. It should help us remember that the beginning is not the end. How well we begin is not the issue; some will start better than others. There will be many things to learn (or unlearn!) that will help us dump the baggage of our old life. It will not happen overnight. Thankfully, God is long-suffering! His love never fails, ever. He will complete the work He begins in us; that is His promise!

Lombardi knew there would be a price to pay for success; there always is. In that first training camp, those eventual Hall of Fame players were a bunch of losers who often thought they were insane for following Vince Lombardi. But there was something about him, a confidence, an assurance that he did not have any doubts about their ultimate success. They were not convinced, but they were convinced he was convinced! He believed in them and they saw that he was committed to making them winners.

For some strange reason, the vast majority of people in the Church do not see the same commitment in the Lord toward us as those Packers believed Coach Lombardi had for them. For some reason, it is not real, it is not intimate, it is not impacting their lives the way it should. Do we not see that Jesus Christ laid down His life for us, even more so than Lombardi laid down his for the Packer players? Jesus was the epitome of the sacrifice and dedication which Lombardi tried to teach the Packers, and to the extent they gave themselves to one another and to him, they began to succeed more and more.

Life was hard those first couple of months, especially in training camp. Some days they thought they were going to die, some days literally! But they kept following Lombardi, listening to him, learning from him, and they began to see the difference, both in their lives and in their team. What was happening? Their faith was growing stronger day by day, game by game.

The Price of Success: Singleness of Purpose

Jesus made this point over and over. He told them you cannot serve God and mammon. You cannot go in two directions at once. You have to make a choice. Isn't this what Jesus told His disciples? Could He have made it any more clear when He said, "If any man wishes to come after Me, let him deny himself daily and take up his cross and follow Me" (Luke 9:23).

In other words: Die. It may sound a little harsh at first, but any superior athlete will tell you it is the only way to achieve ultimate success. In this context, to "die" means to put to death every other competing obstacle, distraction, or affection.

The ultimate key to success at the highest level in sports or in any arena of life is this: *singleness of purpose.* "Keep your eye on the ball." "Keep your head in the game." "Focus!" "Concentrate!" It is really that simple (though the execution is never that simple). The Scriptures teach the same thing.

Do you want to know God? Really know Him? Here is His promise: "You will seek Me and find Me when you search for Me with all your heart" (Jeremiah 29:13). That does not leave room for much else, and that is the point. If the goal is worthy enough, the sacrifices are not a problem.

At the time of this writing, we are heading into the 2014 Winter Olympics. Thousands of skiers, ice skaters, snowboarders, and hockey players will descend on Sochi, Russia to compete against the best athletes in the world in their specialty. For years they have all made tremendous, life-altering sacrifices, often endured great pain and suffering, all for one goal: to compete in the Olympics. They all knew when they started that it would require absolute dedication and strict discipline—and this was just to have the chance to compete! They all love what they do or they could not do it.

Is this how we view God? Is knowing Him really worth the cost? What price are we willing to pay to know Christ? Do we have the desire to sacrifice, if necessary, just to have the chance to truly know Him? Paul makes it clear in his epistle to the Philippians what it meant to him:

> "But whatever things were gain to me, those things I have counted as loss for the sake of Christ. More than that, I count all things to be loss in view of the surpassing value of knowing Christ Jesus my Lord, for whom I have suffered the loss of all things, and count

them but rubbish so that I may gain Christ, and be
found in Him...."   —Philippians 3:7-9a

The Single Purpose of Our Life

God left no room for doubts or questions about what the single,
ultimate purpose of our lives as Christians is to be. It is declared
in both the Old and New Testaments. What is that purpose?

It is to seek Him, to find Him, to love Him and serve Him,
period. The first time we see this clearly stated is in the book of
Deuteronomy. Israel has just spent the last 40 years wandering
in the desert because they refused to trust and obey their God. In
other words, they refused to follow Him and obey Him.

Now, as a new generation is about to cross over into the
Promised Land, God instructs Moses to teach them the
fundamentals once again. There is the one lesson they must
never forget. It is the key to having the blessing of God on their
lives and their children's lives. What is that?

> "Hear, O Israel! The LORD is our God, the LORD is
> one! You shall love the LORD your God with all your
> heart and with all your soul and with all your might.
> These words, which I am commanding you today, shall
> be on your heart. You shall teach them diligently to
> your sons...."   —Deuteronomy 6:4-7a

In the New Testament, when the Lord Jesus is asked what the
greatest commandment is, He quotes this verse. That should
confirm to us how crucial it is. To love and obey God is not
optional. It **is** the path of life. And, it is important to note, this is
not for God's benefit. He does not need our love. It is for our
benefit. We need this relationship with Him if we are to truly

enjoy the life God has given us. It is He who is the key to satisfaction and fulfillment in our lives.

Those who rebel against this command find themselves floundering in life, unable to find joy even when they have apparently succeeded. The stories are endless of those who "rose to the top of their chosen field," only to find there was no real joy, no lasting satisfaction. To fail to seek God with all your heart leaves you vulnerable to all the allurements the world offers, and you will not be able to resist them for long. Why should you, unless you have a greater purpose in life? But to those who seek Him, God's promise to us is certain. Make this your cornerstone in life.

> "You will seek Me and find Me when you search for Me
> with all your heart."   —Jeremiah 29:13

There is a familiar scene in all three of the synoptic gospels (Matthew, Mark, and Luke). It is the Lord's encounter with a scribe (a legal expert in Jewish law). It is the account of a seeker who understood the letter of the law, could even teach others, but was ultimately unwilling to pay the price to follow the Lord himself. The Lord's answer to his question settled the issue.

> "Teacher, which is the great commandment in the
> Law?" And He said to him, "YOU SHALL LOVE THE
> LORD YOUR GOD WITH ALL YOUR HEART, AND
> WITH ALL YOUR SOUL, AND WITH ALL YOUR
> MIND. This is the great and foremost commandment."
>   —Matthew 22:36-38

Again, the absoluteness of the command leaves no room for competing affections. The key word here is "all": *all* the heart, *all* the soul, *all* the mind. That is everything!

Why make this commitment? Is it really worth it? If you are going to love someone with this kind of single-minded, whole-hearted devotion, shouldn't there be some compelling attraction for them? What would make it worth it? Here is the answer: You will know God; the Creator and Sustainer of the universe will reveal Himself to you. He will reveal all that He has done for you already, and all that He plans to do with you throughout the eternity you will spend with Him. His love is unfathomable.

His great desire in creating us was to have this relationship. He has determined, in spite of all our sin and rebellion that He is going to satisfy His desire, no matter what the cost. When you begin to grasp and believe in this love, the more your life will change.

Here is a small example. Consider this amazing truth:

> "For the eyes of the LORD move to and fro throughout the earth that He may strongly support those whose heart is completely His..." —2 Chronicles 16:9

At every moment of every day, God is searching throughout the whole earth, throughout the whole human race, looking for men and women through whom He can manifest His divine power. He wants to reveal Himself to men. Jesus is not here physically on earth any more. The most powerful witness He has on earth is a man or woman whose heart is fixed on seeking Him, loving Him, and serving Him. His power in that life is undeniable and unmistakable; it is Christ. It is the power of God. It is what puts the iron in Iron-Man.

To see this promise fulfilled in your life, the first thing you have to do is truly believe in your coach and be willing to follow him. Hebrews 11:6 says, "...without faith it is impossible to please Him, for he who comes to God must believe that He is and that He is a rewarder of those who diligently seek Him."

The Packers believed in Vince Lombardi—and followed him to victory. Do we rise to that level of faith in our following Jesus Christ? If not, why not?

If you want to win, you have to decide if it is worth it. Are you willing to pay the price? There will be challenges, obstacles, temptations and distractions, but the goal and the reward that we seek is far greater than the Packers could ever win. And it won't just last for a season, it lasts for eternity. Is this what you want?

If so, then you need to consider who your coach will be. He will be the most important person in your life. He will be the one you follow. He will be the one to determine the path on which you travel with him. You need to know that he is an Iron-Man.

There is only one right path and only One who could rightfully say, "Follow Me—I am the way."

Chapter Four

The Coach: Vince Lombardi?
Who Is He? Why Pick Him?

"Winning isn't everything, it's the only thing."
–Vince Lombardi

By 1958 Green Bay had become the Siberian gulag of the NFL (a *gulag* is a place of exile, a place where you go and are not likely to be heard from again!) In Packer history there are stories of players' wives who broke down in tears when they found out their husbands had been traded to the Green Bay Packers. It was widely viewed as a career-ending, death sentence for a professional football player.

The National Football League (NFL) was formed in 1920 with about 14 team franchises. Today there are 32 teams, but only a handful of the original franchises remain. Teams like the New York Giants, the Chicago Bears, and the Detroit Lions are among the survivors. So are the Green Bay Packers.

When you look back at its history, it is kind of an anomaly. It is an ultra-small market team. When Bart Starr first told his wife Cherry that he had been drafted by Green Bay, she said to him, "Honey, where is that?" Then she sighed with quiet disappointment when she saw it on the map. It was a long way from home in Alabama.

In 1958, Green Bay's population was only about 100,000. By contrast, its nearest competitor was the NFL Chicago Bears franchise, which had a population of over 3.5 million to draw from! How could Green Bay hope to compete? A large fan base is crucial to the success of any sports team. Even its nearby southern neighbor, Milwaukee, had a population of over 700,000. Why not move the franchise there?

The truth is, it almost did, several times. Most of the other NFL owners really wanted that move to happen. But Green Bay had one thing the other cities did not have, at least not to the same extent. What was that? A rabidly loyal fan base. The town owned the team, both literally and emotionally as fans. It is actually a public company, owned by the citizens of Green Bay and others who love the Packers. There is no billionaire owner to bankroll the team.

Yet, even though they live in the frozen tundra of Wisconsin winters and have an open air stadium, they have sold out every game since 1960! Their stadium now seats about 80,000, yet their population is only about 250,000. The point is, virtually everyone in Green Bay is a Packers fan. Always have been, always will be. It seems to be in their DNA. There is a waiting list of over 100,000 people waiting to buy season tickets to Packers' games.

And Vince Lombardi knew this. He knew the depth of support he would have if he could turn the Packers into a winning team. Still, why pick Lombardi?

The men in charge of recruiting a new head coach knew that if they did not pick the right man and turn this team around, they would likely lose the franchise to another city. Their first instinct was to hire a big-name coach. In fact, most Packers' fans and players thought they would and should. One former Packer coach and NFL legend, Curly Lambeau, namesake of Lambeau Field in Green Bay, was actively lobbying for the job and seemed to have the inside track since he had been a winning Packers coach in prior years. But as they sought the counsel and advice of some of the most successful NFL franchise owners, one name kept coming up: Vince Lombardi.

A Man Prepared for the Job

To become a head coach for the first time in your life in your mid-40's was unusual. To become the head coach of an NFL football team without ever having been a head coach of anything other than a high school football team was unheard of. It is a bit of a cliché, but Lombardi had, in a very real sense, been preparing for this his whole life.

Lombardi was a smart man. He graduated magna cum laude from Fordham University. He taught high school chemistry, math, and Latin. At Fordham, he became famous as one of the *Seven Blocks of Granite*. At only 5'10" and 175 lbs., it was, as one teammate put it, "his strength and ferociousness" which made him an anchor on a team which captured seven shutouts his final season.

As a high school football coach, he captured six state titles. His great ambition was to coach in college. He got his chance in 1947 when he joined the coaching staff at Fordham. But his big break came two years later when "Red" Blaik, the head coach at Army (West Point), asked him to come join their staff. During the war years, Army was a football powerhouse. Blaik had already won two national football championships and was widely acknowledged as one of the finest coaches in the land. Lombardi, as you would expect, jumped at the chance!

Lombardi was a passionate and dedicated man. He had the ultimate essential of true leadership: singleness of purpose. Lombardi saw this trait as the key to "Red" Blaik's success. He allowed him to mentor him in all aspects of the game, eliminating the superfluous and focusing on the essentials. This had the two-fold benefit of both simplifying his coaching philosophy and also streamlining it. The results were obvious. Wherever he went, Lombardi's teams won!

Green Bay Needed a Difference-Maker

In 1958, the Green Bay Packers were sloppy, undisciplined, and lazy. Most players were in the habit of doing what they wanted to do. Even during games, they would often take themselves out just to rest. And the coaches let them. The lack of organization and discipline was killing the team.

When Lombardi arrived in Green Bay in February, the first thing he did was to sit down with his coaches and look at all the game tapes of the previous losing season. He immediately saw that the big problem was not talent; it was that many of the players did not really seem to care if they won or not. This was an attitude problem. No team can win without players who are there to play to win. Lombardi knew he would have to get rid of a number of players, even talented players, to change the locker room mindset of the Packers. Ultimately, it was the players themselves who decided who should stay and who should go. Lombardi just looked for the ones who would follow him; these were the ones he could transform into winners.

Lombardi was also a tough, disciplined man. He viewed the football field as a war zone. The results were always the same. Either you won or you lost; victory or defeat were the only options. And Vince Lombardi hated to lose. His goal was to instill that hatred of losing into the minds and hearts of his team. At the same time, Lombardi could take a loss if he was convinced that his team had played with all their heart, no reserve.

In order to do this, he had to make sure his teams were in top condition. Their training schedule was agony. Many thought about quitting. But most sensed the rightness of what Lombardi was doing, even if they also thought he was nuts! You could not win and keep winning if your team fizzled in the fourth quarter because their strength failed. All the skill in the world could not save you if that happened. Lombardi built his teams for power and strength. If you were going to beat the Packers, you had to be ready to pay a heavy price. It was not going to be easy ever again.

Lombardi was also a great teacher. What makes a great teacher? *The greatest teachers have the ability to communicate their vision in a way that can be both understood and experienced. In other words, those you teach can make it their own.* This is what coaches mean when they say their players have bought into their scheme; they both understand and believe in the coach's strategy for winning. They are willing to learn it, follow it, and live it.

The players have to believe in what the coach is doing. The proof is in the winning. But there is always a learning curve, a period of trial-and-error learning, where the players have to trust the coach and be willing to follow him, even if they do not see the results immediately.

Lombardi was a supremely confident coach. The players had never heard of him, but those in the upper echelons of NFL management knew exactly who he was. What the players did not know (or care) was that he had been the offensive coordinator for the New York Giants. He coached the offense while Tom Landry (of Dallas Cowboy fame) coached the Giants defense. The head coach of the Giants during that period used to quip that with them coaching the offense and defense, he just had to show up on Sunday and "pump up the balls."

The Giants were perennial contenders under Lombardi's offense. They won the NFL title in 1956 and were second in 1957. Every year he was there, they contended for the title. His offensive system clearly worked. Lombardi was a winner. That was the only measure of success he knew. According to him, that is why they played the game. That is why his most famous quote says what it does:

Winning isn't everything. It's the only thing.

Fifty years ago we would not have to stop and explain this quote —today we do. Lombardi was a deeply religious man. He did not just go through the motions. He went to church every day. His character was a mirror image of his beliefs. Lombardi believed in paying the price to win, but would never embrace winning if it meant compromising his principles or doing anything that represented a less than upright character. Remember, his goal was not just to win, it was the pursuit of perfection.

He did not want to just win, he wanted to dominate his opponents with his team's skill and toughness. He did not want to win by default or by unfair advantage. He wanted to see the other team play their best and beat them at their best! To compromise his integrity in any way just to win a game was unthinkable; it would defeat the whole purpose of playing the game.

This quote needs to be put in perspective by another quote. He once told his brother Joe, "Don't pray for victory, pray for the will of God." At one point, he seriously considered becoming a priest. He believed in God and that, in the end, we all serve Him. Though he led others, he never lost sight of the need to be a follower as well. Lombardi always remembered that God was God and he was not God. He honored God as best he knew how. He knew he needed God's help and He knew one day he would answer to God.

Lombardi was a man of strong character and integrity. These are not words you hear bandied about these days. Sadly, many mindless, unscrupulous politicians have caused a lot of us to be very cynical when we hear those words used to describe a man. But just a generation ago, those words were filled with meaning. Men were judged by their character and behavior, and to fall short in character was a cause for great shame and humiliation. Shame is another word we do not use much anymore. That should really concern us!

Contrast the Modern Standard of Success

Today the supreme issue is **skills**. Can a person perform at the highest level, whether as an athlete, an entertainer, or a CEO? If so, we pay them absurd amounts of money to entertain us or enrich us, then we are routinely subjected to the tales of their lives of excess, blatant immorality, arrogance, and antics that make you want to shake your head in amazement. Most of it is due to giving men of unprincipled character too much praise and too much money too soon. Rarely is it a tale of high moral character.

We had an example of the perils of choosing skills over character in Atlanta just a few years ago. We had a spellbinding quarterback (QB). Every time he got the ball, a shot of electricity went through the crowd. He was a threat to score at any time. Broken plays often became the stuff of highlight reels. The Falcons paid him a mind-numbing sum of $100 million dollars to play for them.

But rather than being a man of wisdom, integrity, and character, he made some really foolish decisions, eventually ending up broke and in prison. He had let "bad company corrupt good morals;" his friends were not true friends at all. He foolishly thought his success gave him special privileges and, ultimately, that he was above the law. He learned some hard lessons. But he did learn.

To his credit, rather than feeling slighted and unfairly treated (i.e., a victim), he humbled himself and accepted the mentorship of some really solid Christian men, true Iron-Men. He now seems to have gotten his life back on track, allowing him to get back on the field. This is another example of one of our basic principles:

"The Beginning is not the End, don't confuse them."

—Wallace Francis

The team that originally drafted him learned a humbling lesson as well. When they went back into the draft to find a new "franchise QB," the first thing they looked for was character and integrity. Skills were still very important, but now they were secondary.

Conclusion

The folks in Green Bay didn't know if Lombardi was the right guy or not. But they kept hearing the testimonies of many of the most respected men in pro football. They all said the same thing. Vince Lombardi is your man. He has the character and integrity you need; he has the knowledge and skills and wisdom you need to turn Green Bay into a winner. He is a winner and he has the passion, the dedication, and discipline to make your team a winner as well.

So they decided to hire Lombardi as head coach. More than that, they gave him full control of the team. He was head coach *and* general manager. For better or for worse, the team was his to mold whatever way he chose. It turned out to be a very wise decision.

The Lesson for Us

We are all going to be on someone's team in life, maybe a number of teams. It may be as a member of a business team, a family team, a ministry team, or an athletic team. There will be leaders for every team, as well as followers. You have to decide if you are going to follow the leader for whatever team you are on. When you decide to follow that leader you need to do it with all your heart and soul. It is a serious commitment which needs careful consideration.

Like Lombardi, a lot of people have heard about Jesus Christ;

they know He lived and died on a cross two thousand years ago, but they do not really know the value of His life and how He can transform their lives. One of the problems is that they do not realize that the self-centered lives they are living now are not the lives of winners, but the lives of losers, eternal losers.

The Lord Jesus asked the question, "What does it profit a man if he gains (i.e., wins) the whole world, but loses his own soul?" We all need to ask ourselves whether the path we are on is simply leading us to gain what we can in this life, but will eventually cost us our soul.

D.L. Moody once said,

"Our greatest fear should not be of failure, but of succeeding at something that doesn't really matter."

That is a sobering statement. How can you avoid making a really bad choice here?

The answer can often be found simply by looking at the "coach" you have chosen to follow. Your life will likely reflect much of his character. What do you see? Is he an Iron-Man? How can you know? How can you evaluate it?

First, you have to assure yourself that the leader or coach you have chosen to follow has true character and integrity. Of course, that also means you have to know what character and integrity are, what they look like in a person, or you will not even know what to look for! Let's think about that because we live in a society that is so obsessed with performance that we have almost lost sight of the importance of character.

What is character? Even more important, what is godly character?

Chapter Five

True Character Commands Respect—It Does Not Demand It

"Knowledge will give you power, but character, respect."

—Martial Artist Bruce Lee

"Most people say that it is the intellect which makes a great scientist. They are wrong: it is character."

—Albert Einstein

We are going to address an issue here that reveals the confusion of many young people today: the difference between that *respect* which is the fruit of upright character and the pseudo-respect that is the result of fear. It is the difference between respect which is "commanded" by strong character and that which is "demanded" by those with weak character or really none at all.

Quite often, especially in movies/TV, we are presented the scene of a young man brandishing a gun at some person who has supposedly "disrespected" them. Of course, we all naturally want respect. But some people feel they are owed respect. If they do not get it, they will take it by force. But what this portrayal is really revealing is that many young people do not understand what real respect is, and they don't want to pay the price to earn it.

Fear is not respect. True respect is admiration for the character of a person. Respect must be earned. It is earned by the living of a life worthy of respect and admiration, especially under difficult, trying circumstances. It is earned by doing good to others, even when it is inconvenient. It is earned by self-sacrifice, by giving oneself to another for their benefit, when there is nothing in it for them. It is the test of character under fire that produces the deepest respect. When the soldier falls on a grenade to protect his "brothers-in-arms," he earns deep, lifelong respect for his selfless action. It takes character to do that.

The man with the gun does not comprehend any of this. We may fear the power of the gun and the one wielding it for a time, but we have no admiration whatsoever for the person who would try to coerce another person into respecting him. That person is not worthy of respect. He proves it by his actions.

Does FedEx Endorse Lying?

As we said earlier, today in America we are so driven by the desire for success that we will make all kinds of excuses for wrong behavior as long as it leads to success in whatever we want to accomplish. Take, for example, lying and cheating. Some experts estimate that up to 80% of us admit to lying! That is a huge number, and it is now to the point we often expect it. It appears to many that lying is now culturally acceptable. Media commercials appear to support this. Just a few years ago, FedEx sponsored a number of commercials which depicted employees lying to their bosses about their plans to play golf. They just outright lied. The tag line from FedEx was, "We understand."

Seriously? The amazing thing is, there did not seem to be any negative response from the public. They seemed to "understand" as well; it was okay to lie in certain situations. After all, nobody got hurt. Again, the morally flexible nature of our culture seems to be okay with this.

There were two or three commercials that had this undercurrent, basically saying that these little "white" lies were somehow justifiable or innocuous and not a big deal. There is no question that the majority of us have lied at some point in our lives. The reality of lying is not in question here. But we never viewed it as anything other than wrong! In God's eyes it is still a sin. Lying reflects a lack of character, an inability or unwillingness to do the right thing even when you might be able to get away with doing the wrong thing.

So it may be that we need to refresh ourselves about what true character is so that we know what we should respect and what not to respect. So let's think about character for a minute.

What Is Character? Why Is It Important?

Character is the sum of the qualities, the principles, and motives that control the direction and the decisions of a person's life. Character reveals who we are and determines what we do. Character is what makes a person "good" or "bad." It reveals the principles and values that have been taught and ingrained in a person's mind and soul. It is the foundation from which they will make their personal decisions and life choices. It is their "code," the rules and principles by which they have chosen to live. It is what enables a person to make the hard choice to do the right thing, even at great personal cost or even loss.

Many do not consciously stop and think about what their core values, their "code" of life is going to be. They just follow the crowd and let others tell them what their "code" should be. They often end up being manipulated by those who have chosen a path which reveals a lack of character, a path which allows them to take advantage of others, to commit some inequity or injustice against them.

Character is simply the revelation of who you really are. Wherever you find good character, you will find integrity alongside it. Integrity is what makes it possible to describe a person as having a "solid character."

What Is Integrity?

Integrity is that part of character which keeps a person from yielding to outside pressure or temptations to compromise their principles and core values in any given situation. Integrity comes from the same root word which gives us the word "integer." An integer is a mathematical term describing a whole number. The numbers 1-2-3 are whole numbers; there is no fractional part to them. It is their wholeness which makes them a good metaphor for character. They are undivided, they are solid and whole, and they won't break or compromise under pressure. You can rely on them to do the right thing, no matter what the situation. They are trustworthy.

The essential character qualities you want to see in your "coaches" in life are moral qualities. Qualities like trust-worthiness, faithfulness, honesty, fairness, justice, kindness, uprightness, selflessness, etc. If you have a leader who lies, cheats, and steals, who compromises to gain unfair advantage over others, has no sense of right and wrong (or is willing to be flexible, depending on the situation), then he or she is not someone you want to follow, even if it looks profitable in the short run. You need to look for an Iron-Man, a man of character and integrity.

Choose Your Coach Carefully—Consider His Path

The Bible is clear on this. Ultimately, there are only two kinds of people in this world: the upright and the wicked. They each follow a different path, and each path leads to its own destination. You cannot change the destination if you stay on the same path.

The book of Proverbs gives multitudes of examples of this. Here are just a few:

> "For the LORD knows the way of the righteous, but the way of the wicked will perish."   —Psalm 1:6

> "The way of the LORD is a stronghold to the upright, but ruin to the workers of iniquity."   —Proverbs 10:29

> "A man who wanders from the way of understanding will rest in the assembly of the dead."—Proverbs 21:16

> "He who pursues righteousness and loyalty finds life, righteousness, and honor."   —Proverbs 21:21

The contrast between the upright and the unrighteous, between those who choose to honor God with their lives and those who choose to live in rebellion, is stark, not subtle. And the difference in their experience in life is just as startling. God is with one; He is not with the other.

But we have an even greater example of what this character should look like. In fact, it is a *perfect* example. So that there might never be a question in our minds, God sent us an example of perfect character, of God-like character, when He chose to send us His Son, the Lord Jesus Christ.

Since God's goal for us is to be transformed and conformed to His likeness with a character just like His, we should know what that means. So what was He like? What was it that drew so many to follow Him? Let's explore that. Who was He?

Chapter Six

A Greater than Solomon

"The Queen of the South will rise up with the men of this generation at the judgment and condemn them, because she came from the ends of the earth to hear the wisdom of Solomon; and behold, something greater than Solomon is here."

—Luke 11:31

The wisdom of Solomon is legendary. His wealth was enormous and his counsel was sought by kings and queens all over the ancient world. The queen of Sheba acknowledged that the people of Israel were blessed to have a king with such wisdom. The whole nation prospered because of his leadership. The people knew it and followed him. Of course, we know that the reason for Solomon's success was the blessing of God.

If you asked the faithful in Green Bay who was greater, King Solomon or Vince Lombardi, there are likely quite a few fans who would choose Lombardi. Of course, that would be silly (we have to remember "fan" is just short for fanatic!). But the reality is Vince Lombardi was revered by the fans in Green Bay. Once he took over, they never had a losing season. The players and the fans truly believed in him. They would follow him anywhere. They knew he had made them winners. What does that tell us?

It tells us that the players and fans in Green Bay (as well as in Israel) were fully capable of recognizing greatness...and smart enough to follow it when they found it! They did not know in the beginning all that they knew at the end of the Lombardi era, but they were willing to learn. They were willing to see IF he was "the one." The more they learned, the more their faith grew. The more they experienced, the more they realized that Lombardi was the one they wanted to follow. They believed that the path he was leading them down was going to result in the success they wanted. They were right.

Now let's apply this to our lives. If you had to choose between following Vince Lombardi (as good as he was) or even King Solomon (as wise as he was) and following Jesus Christ, whom would you choose to follow? Whom would you want to be your "life coach"? Whom would you believe in and trust as your guide?

The obvious answer would be Jesus Christ. And, that is the right answer. But could you truly explain why you want to follow Him? Can you go any deeper than the desire to "be saved"? To have your sins forgiven and a get a "free ticket" to heaven? While understandable (nobody wants to spend eternity in hell), is that really the gospel message? Is that all there is to it? While this may actually be where a good portion of the church is today, if we are to impact this nation (much less the world), this has to change.

Why Do You Follow Anyone?

You usually follow someone for one of two reasons. It may be because they have something in their life that you want in yours; in other words, you want to be like them and believe they can teach you or train you to have what they have. This will require being willing to go where they are going and doing what they do. This is the essence of discipleship, not just in Christianity but in any discipline.

A second reason you might follow someone is because you believe they can do something for you or get something for you that you cannot do or get for yourself. This may be legitimate or it may be a subtle form of idolatry (the essence of idolatry is simply seeking a god to get something for myself. The god's value is purely in what he can do for me).

Lombardi vs. Jesus Christ

To his credit, Coach Lombardi would probably cringe at the idea of being compared in any way to Jesus Christ. But it is also to his credit that the character he demonstrated in his life and the impact of his leadership on so many makes that comparison possible, at least to a point. And, it is important to understand here that this comparison is not a good vs. bad comparison, it is a good vs. the best. So how do they compare?

Lombardi probably thought of his players as sheep at various times. The way he yelled at them, scolded them, ridiculed them and frustrated them with his drive to "do it perfectly," you might think he really did not like them. But that was not true. While this would not qualify him as a good shepherd, he was a good coach who was trying to be a good shepherd. He did some critically important things right. He was with them all the way, he was always looking out for them. He gave himself wholeheartedly for their good and they knew it. They knew they could trust him.

Please do not gloss over that. It is the essence of Christ-likeness. Lombardi was with them and He gave himself for them. The stress of giving himself, literally 18 hours a day, probably cost him an early death. And the players knew it was for their sakes, their benefit, to make them winners.

Isn't this how Paul described the Lord Jesus? As the One who:

> "...loved us and gave Himself up for us, an offering and a sacrifice to God as a fragrant aroma." —Ephesians 5:2

> "...our great God and Savior, Christ Jesus, who gave Himself for us to redeem us from every lawless deed, and to purify for Himself a people for His own possession, zealous for good deeds."
> —Titus 2:13b-14

The Packers saw the sacrifices Lombardi made to make them winners. He was not driving them to greatness, he was leading them there personally. That is what Christ does: He leads us "from victory to victory in the train of His triumph." The Packers became willing followers, willing to pay the price to follow Lombardi to victory. Can we do less if we realize what the Lord Jesus has done for us and to what He is leading us? Wouldn't it be foolish not to?

Lombardi's Limitations

Having said that, even what Lombardi did, he could only do for a small group of men—and there were severe human limitations on that. As bright and imaginative as he was, he was not even as wise as Solomon, much less Jesus Christ. It may be helpful to remind ourselves of some of the differences.

Lombardi undoubtedly gave many stirring pre-game and half-time motivational speeches. He was a gifted public speaker and crowds loved to hear him. But no one has ever compared his speeches to the Sermon on the Mount. Not even close.

Lombardi could motivate men to play through pain and do more than they thought they could achieve, but even he could not tell a crippled man to "rise, take up your bed and walk."

And while the Packers faithful in Green Bay might believe that he caused the Packers franchise to rise from the dead, he did not actually do it. Only Jesus could speak the words that caused Lazarus actually to rise from the dead! And many witnesses saw Him do it.

Likewise, Lombardi was a great teacher, but he could **not** reproduce himself through these men. The Packers learned this the hard way. They won while he was with them, coaching them. But in the 25 years after he left, they won no NFL championships, not one. In fact, they only had five winning seasons in all those years. Even when two of his Hall of Fame players became the head coach of the Packers, they still could not do what Lombardi did, even though they had been so successful with him as players. Lombardi could not reproduce himself in his players.

By contrast, Jesus' disciples received His instruction, were transformed by it, then took the truths of the gospel all over the world and saw the image of Christ reproduced in men and women over and over all over the world! They then committed this message to faithful men who would teach others—the result was that in generation after generation, for over 2000 years, millions (if not billions) of lives have been transformed from selfish, self-centered rebels against God to loyal, faithful servants of Jesus Christ. And the success continues to this day. Lombardi's success pales against the accomplishments of Jesus Christ and those who follow Him.

The question is simple: Whom would you follow? Whom are you following?

You Are Following Someone!

Make no mistake about it, you are following someone now. It may be yourself, it may be someone who has convinced you their path will lead to success. But where does that path end?

Jesus said, "I am the Light of the world; he who **follows Me** will not walk in the darkness, but will have the Light of life" (John 8:12).

He also said, "**I am the way**, and the truth, and the life; no one comes to the Father but through Me" (John 14:6).

The Packers followed Lombardi because they wanted to win football games. That was their goal. *What is your goal?* There is nothing inherently wrong with football games, or wanting to win them. But in the end, they are just that: games. They do not factor into the eternal realities of life.

Let's put it another way. When judgment day comes for those Hall of Fame Packers, including Coach Lombardi, Bart Starr, Jerry Kramer and the rest, God will not be asking a single one of them the question, "How many games did you win?" The only issue will be whether or not it was God's will that they be playing on that team and, if so, whether they did it with all their hearts for His glory, not for their own glory. Again, let's remind ourselves of Moody's sobering message:

> *"Our greatest fear should not be of failure, but of succeeding at something that does not really matter."*

This needs to be part of the decision-making process in determining whom you will follow. Is the path you are going down or about to go down God's choice or yours? Does it really matter? If it is your choice, there may be years of lost opportunities to glorify God—and maybe much worse.

You can deceive yourself about your motivation, but you cannot deceive God. He sees right into our hearts. Your answer is critical, it has eternal significance. The Lord Himself said,

> "Not everyone who says to Me, 'Lord, Lord,' will enter the kingdom of heaven, but he who does the will of My Father who is in heaven." —Matthew 7:21

What is Your Real Goal in Life?

It should be clear that it is crucially important whom we choose to follow, and know where he is going and why we want to follow him. In the case of Jesus Christ, the answer is clear. We follow Him because we believe He is the only one who can lead us back to God the Father—and that is the real goal: to know God, intimately and personally. The Son knows the Father—intimately. He (and only He) can take us to the place where we can know God ourselves. Only Jesus has the divine stamp of approval on His life and is, therefore, acceptable to God. He alone can lead us back to the Father. All other roads lead to destruction, not to the true knowledge of God.

But choosing to follow Christ is really not a difficult decision for those who truly want to seek God. The reason is that there really are no other options! The life which Christ lived was so totally different from any other, there is really no competition and should be no confusion. The Father acknowledged this fact several times.

On the mountaintop when the disciples were given a taste of the glory of Christ, God the Father said to Peter, James, and John, "This is My beloved Son, listen to Him!" (Mark 9:7). If you want to have an eternal relationship with God, Jesus is the only way. Some may believe that this is narrow-minded and not politically correct, but it is biblically accurate. Ultimately, why should we follow Him?

Because He is Worthy!

> "Worthy are You, our Lord and our God, to receive glory and honor and power; for You created all things, and because of Your will they existed, and were created."   —Revelation 4:11

Why follow the Lord Jesus? Because He is worthy of being followed. Because the life He lived was a true revelation of the character and glory of God. He was sinless, he was a perfect man, and he was what God intended man to be like when He created him. Jesus Christ embodied the divine standard of righteousness in His life. What is that standard? Perfection. He was "spotless...and...blameless." But when He offered Himself as a substitute for us, His sacrifice of His life was acceptable to God. How do we know this? We know this because God raised Him from the dead and seated Him at His right hand in Heaven.

Let's think about what Christ was like. What makes Him so unique? The answer is, in one sense, very simple; on the other hand, it is incomprehensible.

He is both God and man—and He will be for all eternity. How can that be? The answer (which we can barely begin to understand) is what makes Him so worthy of our determination to follow Him.

Chapter Seven

The Character of Christ

"Example is not the main thing in influencing others.
It is the only thing."
—Albert Schweitzer

The Packers saw the character and integrity of Vince Lombardi. They saw the real key which moved them to follow him. What was that? They saw that everything he was doing was for their sakes! He was working diligently, tirelessly for one goal: to make them winners. Pay attention to this!

This is the defining character quality of the ultimate Iron-Man coach: His work is all focused on equipping and enabling his players to perform at the highest level. In other words, his life is given so that theirs might succeed; his selfless sacrifice makes it possible for others to achieve things in life they never could have achieved. You might want to read this again—maybe even memorize it.

If anyone ever epitomized this leadership quality, it was Jesus Christ. Why? Because even though He was God (omnipotent, omniscient and co-equal with the Father), He humbled Himself by coming to this earth as a man (laying aside all the privileges and powers that were His as God) that He might bring us back to God. To be sure, this is an almost incomprehensible truth! Yet, the Bible declares it to be so:

> "...although He existed in the form of God, did not regard equality with God a thing to be grasped (i.e., held on to), but emptied Himself, taking the form of a bond-servant...."　　　　　　—Philippians 2:6-7a

How Far Would You Go to Help Someone You Loved?

This is not a perfect analogy, but it will help us get the idea. Let us assume that you really loved dogs (or cats, if you are a cat-lover). And, let's assume they all have a terrible, terminal disease—and it is going to destroy all the dogs/cats in the world. And, let's assume that you can cure that disease. How?

By becoming a dog or cat yourself and giving them a transfusion of your own superior human-dog blood, which will then be turned into an antidote for the disease. The only catch is, if you do this, you will always be a human in the form of a dog. You will be unable to ever change back. You can save those you love, but it will require an enormous, everlasting sacrifice on your part. Would you do it?

Most of us could not fathom doing this, even though we might truly love our pets. The cost of the sacrifice is too great. The humiliation would be too great. Apologies to the PETA folks, but pets are just not people. Jesus did not come to die for the sins of our pets. But He did come to die for ours. And in that coming, he endured suffering and humiliation far beyond what I have described here. This is what the theologians call the Incarnation; it is what the apostle John described as "the Word becoming flesh and dwelling among us" (John 1:14).

But the Scriptures say that "...for the joy set before Him endured the cross, despising the shame..." (Hebrews 12:2). He despised the shame. What a statement! It was shameful what He endured. But He did not let the shame stop Him. He knew that the Cross was essential if the Father's loving desire to save mankind from their sins was to be realized. This was the key to His life and its success: *satisfying the desire of His Father's heart was the most important goal in His life*. It was the guiding force in His life. The gospel of John is a testament to this.

Jesus never ceased being God. But when He became man, becoming the mediator between God and man, something changed forever in the second person of the Trinity. He was now the God-Man. He now had a "body," a people who are so united with Him in Spirit that the Bible says they are "one with Him." They are His people—and will be for all eternity. What a salvation! What a Savior!

Recovering Lost Truths

It should be clear by now that the primary purpose of this little book is to encourage all who read it to be convinced that the only sure path to success in life is to determine in our hearts, once and for all, to follow Him, to learn of Him, to trust Him completely with our lives. This is living faith.

The reasons we should do so are many. The Scriptures which testify to it are everywhere. But there is one truth that is foundational to all the others. Jesus Christ is God in human form. Today many deny that truth. Many even doubt the existence of God at all.

The sad reality today is that we have a whole generation of young people who have been taught that to believe in God and only one God, to believe that He created this world and that we are accountable to Him, is a sign of gross ignorance and foolishness. They hold those who believe such things in derision, as simpletons who deserve no respect. They despise them just as they despised the Lamb of God. Romans 1 says that those who believe these lies are the real fools, even though they think they are wise.

It is time to raise up a generation of young people who know the truth and who know who the real fools are—and are willing to, like their Lord, despise the shame and scorn the ridicule that they might incur when they stand up to them. Are we the fools for trusting in Christ or are they the fools for not believing in Him? One of us is right and the other is wrong. *The game clock is winding down.* It is time to decide what team we are on.

The Biblical Testimony

But what does the Bible say about Jesus Christ? Here again, you have to settle the issue in your own mind whether you believe that the Bible is really a book of truth; that it is the infallible, inerrant word of God. If so, then God has given you an enormous amount of truth to convince and assure you that believing in and following Jesus Christ is the wisest, most intelligent decision you can ever make. If you do not believe it, you are left with the vain reasonings of sin-polluted minds which, according to the Bible, can only lead you down the path of destruction. The choice is yours. But you need to make it wisely and prudently with all the facts.

Here is what the Bible says about Jesus Christ: He is the perfect representation of God's nature. In other words, in Jesus we see what God's character looks like in a human being. In

Hebrews 1:1-3 it says, "God...in these last days has spoken to us in His Son...the radiance of His glory and the exact representation of His nature, and upholds all things by the word of His power."

God dwelling in human flesh! Isn't this a contradiction in terms? Normally, we would have to say this is simply impossible, it cannot happen. All that we know about God and His attributes argues against it. How is it possible? This is the mystery of the Incarnation, that God became flesh.

But the Bible says,

> "In the beginning was the Word, and the Word was
> with God, and the Word was God...the Word became
> flesh and dwelt among us, and we beheld His glory,
> glory as of the only begotten from the Father...."
>
> —John 1:1, 14

Let's put it this way. If God the Father, the Ancient of Days, the eternal God, the God of Abraham, Isaac, and Jacob, the God who raised Jesus from the dead and glorified Him with Himself in heaven...if He were Himself to take on human form and stand next to Jesus, you could not tell them apart.

This is why when Philip asked Jesus to "show us the Father," Jesus responded saying,

> "Have I been so long with you, and yet you have not
> come to know Me, Philip? **He who has seen Me has seen
> the Father...."** —John14:9

Paul also goes into great detail in Philippians 2 emphasizing this truth, how important it is to God and how it should motivate us in following Him. Here is what Paul said,

> "Have this attitude in yourselves which was also in Christ Jesus, who, although He existed in the form of God, did not regard equality with God a thing to be grasped, but emptied Himself, taking the form of a bond-servant, and being made in the likeness of men. Being found in appearance as a man, He humbled Himself by becoming obedient to the point of death, even death on a cross."   —Philippians 2:5-8

This is what Jesus did. Theologically, this is one of the most profound passages in all the New Testament. The totality of what is being revealed is truly beyond our comprehension. We cannot grasp what it means for an infinite, omnipotent, holy God to lay aside the glory which is His as God, to come to earth, be clothed in human flesh, humble Himself and willingly become obedient to His Father, determining to do His Father's will, even though that meant dying on the cross for our sins. It is a staggering reality! There is really no way we can grasp it all.

But the Father knew what it meant and that, as Paul says, is why He "highly exalted Him." When Jesus came to this earth as a man, the miracle of the Virgin Birth meant that, in the person of Jesus Christ, God and man were joined together—forever! When He ascended to Heaven after His resurrection, He ascended as the God-man. His humanity was now permanently part of His deity. This made it possible for those who would decide to "follow Him" to be "one with Him." In honor of completing this work for His Father, God made His Son "Lord" of all. Though much of the world lives in rebellion against Him today, God has determined that one day every tongue will confess that He is indeed Lord, rightful ruler of all.

This was the essence of the Apostle Peter's message to the

crowd on the day of Pentecost.

> "Therefore let all the house of Israel know for certain that God has made Him both Lord and Christ—this Jesus whom you crucified." —Acts 2:36

And Paul said in Romans 14:

> "For not one of us lives for himself, and not one dies for himself; for if we live, we live for the Lord, or if we die, we die for the Lord; therefore whether we live or die, we are the Lord's. For to this end Christ died and lived again, that He might be Lord both of the dead and of the living." —Romans 14: 7-9

It is God's ultimate plan. By being saved from our sins, and by being made one with Him through the new birth, we become children of God and citizens of God's new kingdom, where Christ is Lord of all.

The only question is: Will we hear and obey God's call to "follow Him"? You have to decide once and for all.

Chapter Eight

Choosing to Follow Christ

"Therefore I urge you, brethren, by the mercies of God, to present your bodies a living and holy sacrifice, acceptable to God, which is your spiritual service of worship. And do not be conformed to this world, but be transformed by the renewing of your mind...."

—Romans 12:1-2a

It is a choice. Every elite athlete, college or professional, knows that when he signs the contract agreeing to play for a team, his life as he has known it is over. That is simply the nature of true commitment. There are new rules which will govern their lives and they agree to play by those rules.

But it is a choice they make willingly! They are glad and delighted to make that commitment. It is a day of celebration! They are going to reap huge rewards that they could have no other way. They do not see it as anything other than a huge opportunity!

Here Is the Reality:
Choosing to Follow Christ Is Also a Choice

A life-ending choice! It is a choice to end a life of disobedience and rebellion against God Almighty and choosing to follow Christ. The Scriptures are clear: the same requirement is laid down in each of the synoptic gospels,

> "If anyone wishes to come after Me, he must deny himself, and take up his cross and follow Me. For whoever wishes to save his life will lose it; but whoever loses his life for My sake will find it. For what will it profit a man if he gains the whole world and forfeits his soul? Or what will a man give in exchange for his soul?" —Matthew 16:24-26

> "If anyone wishes to come after Me, let him deny himself, and take up his cross daily and follow Me." —Luke 9:23

There is no question that these verses clearly describe a life-ending decision. The "cross," as we all know, was the means by which Jesus was executed. The Romans used it as a very public (and very effective!) means of discouraging disobedience to Roman law. When Roman soldiers arrived at your door and told you to take up your cross, it meant that your life was about to end. You would put that crossbar on your shoulders and carry it to the place where you would be crucified. Everyone who saw you knew what was happening. That was the point.

But here is the difference. In the verses above, the one who chooses to follow Jesus is voluntarily accepting the cross; he wants to take it up. Why would a person do that? Because he now realizes the benefits and rewards are far greater than the cost of the dead-end life he is leaving behind. Like the elite athlete, it should be a day of rejoicing and celebration. The excitement of a dream fulfilled, an incredible new opportunity should permeate the decision!

Obviously, you are not going to make this decision lightly. Like the elite athlete, you understand you are going to begin to play by different rules now. Someone else is being given the right to rule your life. Someone else is going to set your priorities now. Someone else is going to train you how to achieve your ultimate goals.

Why would you do this? Why would you willingly let someone else control your life?

You would have had to come to a great realization: My way does not work! The path I am on does not lead where I thought it did and the consequences are catastrophic!

The Great Realization: I am Going the Wrong Way!

The day a person's eyes are opened to the reality of what the Bible tells us is our great problem is both a great relief and a cause for great fear. What does the Bible say? Isaiah 53:6 puts it this way: "All of us like sheep have gone astray, each of us has turned to his own way...."

What does he mean? Sheep are notoriously dumb animals. They need a shepherd, both to guide them and to protect them. Without a shepherd, they will wander all over the place and usually get into trouble. The Bible says that is what we are like. Ever since Adam chose to disobey God in the Garden of Eden (a really dumb decision, considering what he had going there!), men have chosen to go their own way, ignoring and disobeying God's commandments. We lie, we steal, we covet, we lust, and we dishonor our parents, all to satisfy our own selfish desires. Anything but submit to God's will. This is what "going our own way" means.

But it is the wrong way! We are on what Jesus calls the "broad way," it is the path to destruction and hell. Paul puts it bluntly in Romans 3, quoting from passages all over the Psalms. He weaves a rather bleak picture of our "relationship status" with God. It is not that of a "BFF" (for you older folks, "BFF" stand for Best Friends Forever)! Scripture says we are enemies, not friends.

Paul concludes that among all mankind:

> "...[T]here is none righteous, not even one; there is none who understands, there is none who seeks for God; all have turned aside, together they have become useless; there is none who does good, there is not even one.... The path of peace they have not known. There is no fear of God before their eyes."   —Romans 3:10-12, 17-18

The key thing to note in these verses is Paul's incessant use of the words "all" and "none"! He is relentless! He does not leave any wiggle room. The whole human race is in a desperate situation. There are no good people! All have sinned and fallen short of the glory of God. There are no exceptions! None! Not even one!

The breach between God and man because of our disobedience is an insurmountable barrier, not because God is mad at us, but because men *refuse* to abandon the path they are on. Think about what these verses say.

No man is righteous. No man can stand before God and present Him a life which was lived in moral perfection, for Him and for His glory. No man even understands the problem and the need to seek God's help! We have all (note that: "all") turned off the path of righteousness and are living our lives for our pleasure and satisfaction. Because we have chosen to do this, we are "useless" to God. Why?

Because the purpose for our lives cannot be fulfilled as long as we are living in rebellion against Him. Most people live lives of perpetual turmoil and never know a life lived on "the path of peace." The bottom line is, as Paul says, "There is no fear of God before their eyes." Something has to change or this life will end in disaster and failure.

The Bible calls this turning, this complete change of direction: repentance. It is a day of decision.

"Signing Day"

All over the nation, usually sometime in early spring, the NFL holds their annual draft. The teams choose the player they want, and he either signs a contract with them or waits until the next year. A few will "hold out," trying to negotiate more lucrative deals, but most are just delighted to get to play "pro ball." In college, it is a little different.

In the NCAA, colleges hold what they call "signing day." It is a day of decision and commitment for high school players. Colleges only have so many scholarships they can award to elite high school athletes. This is the day when the most highly-rated prospects are expected to make the decision as to where they will play. The coaches have all made their offers and appeals trying to convince the players which direction they should go. It is decision time.

It is the day when these young players will decide not only which school they want to play for, but which Coach they want to learn from and follow and what path they believe is likely to lead them to the greatest success.

But it is also a day when they decide which path they will *not* go down, which schools and which coaches they will not follow and play for. You cannot play on two teams at once; you have to make a choice. It is very much like those traditional wedding vows which say "forsaking all others" and making a life-time commitment to one person alone.

A similar day occurs in the life of every Christian. Head Coach Jesus Christ has sent His ambassadors throughout the whole world making the offer and appeal to join His "team." It is a day of decision. It is a day when we decide whether we think the opportunity to be on His team is worth the cost of "turning from" the path we are on.

Repentance and faith are how we make that turn and begin the journey of being on God's team and following Christ. He has promised we will be delivered from both the penalty and the power of sin; we will be changed and empowered to begin to live a whole new life which will result in our becoming conformed to the image of Christ. Do we believe Him?

It is a life-long process. It is a big, life-altering decision. The rewards are huge, but once we make the decision there is no turning back. Therefore, we should be clear about what it all means. In other words, as Luke 14:28 exhorts us, we need to count the cost.

Repentance and Faith

In biblical terms, repentance means a "change of mind." Jesus, Peter, and Paul all declared the necessity of repentance if we are to receive the forgiveness of our sins. Jesus said, "Unless you repent, you will perish." Beware of those who would try to make repentance a mere intellectual act, something we say we believe, but results in no action. Biblical repentance results in a change of mind which always leads to a change of action, a change of direction or a change of purpose. The power to change will be part of God's gift of His Holy Spirit in salvation.

It is simply not possible to truly change our mind about something and it not result in a change of action. It is the way we are wired. We act on what we believe.

The Bible also uses the terms "turn from" and "turn away" to describe the same concept. If I am worshiping idols (i.e., something or someone other than the one, true God), then come to the understanding that this is wrong and turn away from worshiping the false god to worship the true God, I have repented. I changed my mind about whom I should worship and serve with my life and it resulted in a change of action.

To prepare the way for the coming of Jesus Christ as the Messiah, the Savior of the world, John the Baptist came preaching a baptism of repentance. He preached against sin and disobedience to God's laws. If men were to be forgiven their sins, there would have to be a radical change of mind. They would have to see that their lives were being lived in disobedience and rebellion against God, that they had violated His divine laws. There were consequences to their choices.

They would have to come to the realization that they were rightfully accountable to God and that their guilt and judgment were just. Their only hope was to turn from their rebellion and seek His forgiveness. When they came to John for baptism, they were acknowledging their sin and guilt and seeking God's forgiveness—and doing it publicly. They were acknowledging they were guilty as charged and needed God's mercy. The same is true for us.

*　　*　　*　　*　　*　　*

Paul described this same experience in even fuller terms in Acts 20:20-21 when he described his message and ministry to the Ephesian elders. He said that he had not "shrunk from declaring anything that was profitable...teaching them publicly and from house to house." What was his message? "...Solemnly testifying to both Jews and Greeks of <u>repentance</u> toward God <u>and</u> <u>faith</u> in our Lord Jesus Christ." Repentance and faith were the essentials needed for salvation.

This does not mean that these people would never sin again. Unfortunately, that is not possible—for any of us. We all still have a sinful nature. But it does mean that with all our heart we desire to turn from a life of rebellion against God and seek to follow the Lord, living our lives for His glory. But repentance only gets you part of the way to God.

Now, your real need is exposed. You need the *power* to live a different life!

Repentance does not save you, it only gets you to the place where God can show you His solution to your need. As you "turn from" your sin and rebellion, you need someone or something to "turn to." God's answer is His Son. God's answer is the One that John the Baptist said was "the Lamb of God" who takes away the sin of the whole world. The answer is to believe in the Lord Jesus Christ (Acts 16:31). This faith leads to much more than just the forgiveness of our sins!

What is Saving Faith?

Faith is Trust. It is that simple. We all know what trust is. Trust is when your father says to you as a young child that if you jump in the pool, he will catch you. Even though you cannot swim yet, you can trust your father to keep you from drowning. So you jump. You have entrusted yourself to another to keep you from harm. And you are saved from drowning. That is saving faith.

By placing our trust in what Jesus did on the Cross, two things happen. First, our sin and guilt is wiped away. The Lord Jesus died in our place to satisfy the wrath of God against our sin; our sin is wiped away...forever! Here is God's promise: "As far as the east is from the west, So far has He removed our transgressions from us" (Psalm 103:12).

Please note what this verse says: He **has** removed our transgressions from us, not He **will**. It is done. In the dying words of Our Lord, "It is finished." In the mind of God, the issue was settled from before the foundation of the world. To reap this blessing, all that was needed was our repentance and faith. The penalty is paid.

Please note that the verse says "He" has done this. We have no part in this. It is a divine decision to take away our sins and put them in a place where they will never be remembered. No human action can undo what God has done. We can refuse to believe He has done it, but we cannot undo what He has done. If we keep bringing our past back up, telling ourselves how we have failed, that conversation is only going on between you and the devil; God has no part in it.

But there is still something lacking. We need power, spiritual power, to live this changed life.

The Divine Do-Over: "You Must Be Born Again."

Our sins are forgiven; the barrier between us and God is no longer there. However, there still remains a deep divide, a chasm that we in ourselves cannot bridge. What is the problem? We have no power to live a different life. We need a new source of life. We are declared righteous, now we need the ability to *do* righteousness, or as 1Peter 1:15 says, "Be holy yourselves...."

God knew this. He knew there could be no living, intimate relationship with Him by simply dealing with our sin. What we lacked, what was so polluted in us by sin, was the desire, the heart to love and serve Him. Jesus told Nicodemus that the ultimate solution, the only solution, would mean we would have to be born again (John 3).

A "new birth"? How could that be? How could a man be born again? The same miraculous power, the Holy Spirit of God, that allowed a virgin named Mary to conceive a sinless Son would have to work a miracle in us. To accomplish this, God sent His Holy Spirit at Pentecost.

The Holy Spirit is the source of our new life. He is the power of God unto salvation (Romans 1:16); He is the One who makes us "one spirit" with the Lord (1 Corinthians 6:17), the One who seals us in Christ forever. He is the One who reveals the mind of Christ and the things of God to us. He is the bridge that makes an intimate relationship with a holy God possible again. He is Christ in us (Colossians 1:27). He is the power of God in us that enables us to be conformed and transformed into the image of Christ (Romans 8:29; 12:1-2).

He is the advantage that Vince Lombardi never had. Lombardi could teach and train and try to motivate his players, but he could not be in them. He could prepare them, inspire them, but he could not be the power in them to succeed. God has done this for us in Christ. He has "caused us to be born again," to have new hearts and minds that can be transformed by truth and a new spirit which enables us to enjoy intimate fellowship with Him once again.

*   *   *   *   *

All this is made possible for us by God. The only question is, have you "signed on" with God's team? Have you chosen your coach, your master teacher? In the truest sense, you are becoming a disciple of Christ. It was the disciples who were first called Christians (Acts11:26).

The term "Christian" is used only three times in the entire New Testament. The term used to describe the followers of Christ is "disciple" and it is used 240+ times! That should tell us something about where the emphasis of New Testament teaching is aimed. Those who believed followed Christ.

Some would try to convince us that you can believe in Christ for salvation and then, at some later, more convenient time, decide to follow Him as a disciple. To such a foolish idea, I would suggest four things.

First, it is the complete opposite of the entire presentation of the lives of those in the New Testament who followed Christ.

Second, even if you were truly saved and tried to live your life on this basis, it simply will not work. Your life will be one of endless frustration with God. You will be living your life for your sake, trying to achieve personal satisfaction and success when God expects you to live for His sake and do His will! The simple fact is, Christ does not come without a cross in your life.

Third, the only reason a person would want to be "saved," but not want to wholeheartedly commit to following Christ is because he or she still wants to walk on the "old path" and continue to enjoy the world as he or she once did. In other words, he or she refuses to repent. This is simply not biblical Christianity.

Fourth, the one man whom the Scriptures record who waited for a "more convenient time" to become a Christian (Festus), apparently ended up in hell. Not a wise move.

In 1 Corinthians 5:15, Paul is clear about the terms of our contract: "...and He died for all, so that they who live might no longer live for themselves, but for Him who died and rose again on their behalf."

You can't play on God's team without this kind of attitude. The question for us is this, will we hear and obey His call? Will we follow Him? Are we willing to "lay down our lives"? The Packers did it for Vince Lombardi. Can we do any less for the Lord Jesus Christ?

C.T. Studd was one of God's choice Iron-Men. For those who have not heard of him, C.T. Studd was a graduate of Cambridge University in the 1880's. He was one of the most heralded college athletes of his day in England. His honors and awards in England were on the same order there as the Heisman Trophy is in America today. He was born into great wealth and privilege, but upon graduation he gave it all up to follow Christ and join Hudson Taylor in the evangelization of China. His decision and testimony to multitudes of college students all over England began a student revival. The quotes below reveal how clearly and simply he viewed the issue of following Christ.

> *"If Jesus Christ be God and died for me, then no sacrifice can be too great for me to make for Him."*

> *"Only one life, 'twill soon be past; only what's done for Christ will last."*

Do we see the truth in his words? This is what the Bible calls a "new heart" (Ezekiel 36:26), a heart which loves God and others more than oneself. To live and love like this requires a supernatural act of God, but this is exactly what the gospel promises to those who are born again.

Once the decision to follow Christ is settled, it is time to learn how to play on God's team. Again, the Packers' experience provided a great example; they had to learn how to play for Lombardi.

Section Two

The Team

The Players and Coaches:

Their Roles and Strategies to Win

Chapter Nine

What Do I Do Now?

"God isn't looking for people of great faith, but for individuals ready to follow Him."—J. Hudson Taylor

Plese read that quote again. It was made by a man who faced impossible odds. How could anyone hope to share a life-changing message with a people who viewed him, literally, as a "foreign devil"? The answer was simple. Believe God and follow Him in obedience. Hudson Taylor did, and now there are a hundred million Chinese Christians. When we follow the right coach, amazing things can happen.

Once the decision is made and an athlete signs the contract to join a team, it is up to the head coach to tell him what to do next. In college or in the professional ranks, this will all be addressed by the team office. They will tell him when to report to camp and what he is expected to do. Why? In the words of the apostle Paul, "You are not your own...you have been bought with a price" (1Corinthians 6:20). From now on, he has a new authority in his life. It is their responsibility to tell him what they want him to do for them. He is their servant—often a highly paid one, but a servant nevertheless.

When we think of this from the viewpoint of a Christian

following Christ, it is much the same. In this section of the book we want to address the various player positions and the roles they are expected to fulfill on both offense and defense. It is important to understand how things are put together if we are going to fill our roles successfully.

First, we need to remind ourselves that this is God's Team and, like the Packers did Lombardi, give Him full control of our lives. God has made Jesus Christ Lord. He is now our Head Coach and General Manager. He runs the team. He has the "game plan" and knows the strategy, the only strategy that will win. What He needs now is players who will learn and execute His game plan. Properly executing His game plan will result in multitudes of lost souls being brought into His Kingdom, to love Him, serve Him, and glorify Him.

Second, everyone on the team has a part to play, a specific position to fill. The Bible tells us He has given each of us a special spiritual gift which will enable us to execute our role successfully. We need to understand the position God has given us and fulfill that role—for the team's sake.

The *Body* of Christ Works Like a Team

God compares His team to a human body. Like a team, the body operates as a unit, with each part having a specific purpose to fulfill in the body. It is imperative that every part fulfill its role if the body is to function the way it should.

Some parts appear to have more glory, more importance than others. But this is an illusion; the coach knows better. In the body, the mouth, the hands, the feet, the legs, the eyes, and ears all seem to have the more prominent roles. This is what people see most often, but this is just the outward appearance.

The underlying reality is often quite different. The body is designed to allow us to move quite quickly, to run—and run fast if we need to. However, many of us have heard the awful "snap" signaling a bad strain or tear in the long tendon in our lower back calf. It is the Achilles tendon and goes all the way to our heel. Without this tendon functioning properly we cannot move, we only hobble. You never see this tendon, but if it is injured or does not function properly, you cannot win any races. You vividly (and immediately) see the results when it does not work!

Likewise, while the muscles in the body may have acquired great strength and stamina through diligent training and exercise, we all know that a microscopic virus or infection can drain away all the vitality in the body, sometimes for weeks at a time. Some may even kill us. That is what a plague does. Only when all the members are fulfilling their roles can the body function and perform at the highest level.

In the spiritual body, the body of Christ (which we call the Church), every member has a role to fulfill. The Holy Spirit has gifted us for that role. For some, the gifts and roles are obvious; for others intense training and development are required. Some will have more than one gift or spirit-empowered ability, others will have only one. God, in His infinite wisdom, has designed it this way, including our specific part in His plan.

The point to remember is that God is *not* making up the "game plan" as He goes along. It was all determined and settled before the foundation of the world. He knows the plans He has for each one of us. He knows exactly what position He wants us to play. If we all fill the role that He assigns us and execute the strategy as He has designed it, it is guaranteed to succeed. We will win! The team will win!

The key question is, will we choose to do His will? And also, how do we do this? Here is how Lombardi did it.

Understanding the Big Picture: The Team Strategy

When Lombardi first took over the Packers, He spent weeks looking over team films of the previous year's games. One of the problems he saw was that some of the players had talents that could better be used in different positions. Some had to make adjustments. But the key change was the transition from a primarily pass-oriented offense that incorporated some running plays to a primarily power-running offense which opened up strategic passing opportunities. The players had to *understand* the strategy, *believe* in the strategy, and *execute* the strategy—if they were going to win.

The same is true of the defense. Only by understanding the other team's offensive strategy can you plan and execute an effective defense. This takes time, effort, and commitment. The idea that a Christian can show up on "game day" (Sunday church) and function effectively is as ridiculous as the players on the Green Bay Packers thinking they could just show up on Sunday without any game preparation work and win. It is not going to happen for them and it will not happen for us.

If players had tried to do that with Vince Lombardi, they would have been released from the team...quickly! If you were not ready to give 100%, Lombardi did not want you around the team. You would affect the morale of the others who were giving their all. Lombardi would not tolerate this. He was there to win—and assumed you were also.

As we will see, winning is going to require dedication, discipline, and commitment from the whole team. The offense and the defense both had to fulfill their roles. In the early days of football, it was not unusual at all to find players playing **both** offense and defense. They had a name for this. It was called Iron-Man football. The reality is that true Christianity is very much like Iron-Man football.

Iron-Man Football: the Single-Platoon Era

Most of us have forgotten (or were too young to know) that it was not until the early 1960's that NCAA college football rules permanently allowed *unlimited* player substitutions during any play in the game. Why is that important? It completely changed the game!

Prior to this (except for the WWII era) only limited substitutions were allowed and this resulted in most players having to play both offense and defense. Needless to say, that idea is really unthinkable today, but back then it was the norm. It was expected that most players had to learn the skills necessary to play one offensive position and one defensive position. Some pretty famous players played both ways. Here is one great example.

In the early days, a Hall-of-Famer named Sammy Baugh played quarterback for the Washington Redskins. He was a spellbinding, awesome quarterback. What most people forget is that he also played defensive back and was the Redskins punter. The amazing thing is that he was a top-flight performer at every position. In 1943, he led the league in passing, punting (45.9-yard average), and interceptions (11)!

One of Baugh's more memorable single performances was when he threw four touchdown passes **and** intercepted four passes in a single game against the Detroit Lions. Needless to say, no one has ever done that again!

Sammy Baugh was one of the first players inducted to the NFL Hall of Fame in its inaugural year in 1963. He was inducted with all-time greats like Bronco Nagurski, Jim Thorpe, Red Grange, and Curly Lambeau (for whom Lambeau Field in Green Bay is named). If you want a really interesting Google exercise, google Sammy Baugh. He was the epitome of Iron-Man football.

Christianity is like *Iron-Man* football. On God's team, we all have to be ready to play both offense and defense. He will train us and equip us to do what He needs us to do to win. He will "coach us up" so that we are ready to play and play to win. Like any game, it is going to have its grueling moments. But as Christians, we have to be prepared. The stakes could not be any higher. The eternal souls of men are at stake. We play to win! God's promise is that the gates of hell will not prevail against us.

My Personal Testimony

When I first came to the Lord I had no idea what He had planned for me. I knew my life was taking a new direction because He was leading me to leave professional football. Needless to say, everyone (especially my family) thought I was crazy, I was at the peak of my career. All-American and two-time Pro Bowl quarterback Steve Bartkowski was throwing me passes, and the Atlanta Falcons had serious playoff potential. I could be a part of a winning team.

But I had "signed on" with the Lord. I was on His team now, so I declined the contract with the Falcons. It was a costly decision. But I was the Lord's now and I needed Him to direct me. He was my head coach and the first thing I needed to know was Him...intimately.

This is a truth that is often missed by young followers of Jesus Christ. They are anxious to **do** something for the Lord, rather than **be** something to the Lord. They are grateful for His saving work in their lives and excited by the opportunity to be used to save others. After all, there is a whole world to be saved. Right? Yes and no. The Lord has called us *first* to Himself, *then* to His service.

If we miss this point (and many do), if we miss the need to have a deep, intimate relationship with Him, we will be vulnerable to the enemy's attacks when we get into the real battles, the battles for souls. And we will often find ourselves struggling to maintain the motivation and strength to fight when things really get tough. And be sure of this, at some point they will get really tough!

Knowing what I needed, the Lord sent me to a small Bible school in South Carolina[1] to study under a man who (as I look back) was much like Vince Lombardi. He was tough, but fair. He loved the Lord with all his heart and he expected the same from me. He held up high standards. It seemed some days like he expected nothing less than perfection. Why? He said Jesus Christ deserved nothing less. After all, didn't He "love you and give Himself for you?" Didn't He lay down His life for us? Of course, he was right. How could I do less? How could any of us?

I learned many lessons during that season of study, but the main lesson was the need to know my Lord—deeply and intimately. Next, I had to master His truths and understand His plans, both for me and for my ministry for Him.

*   *   *   *   *

In the next few chapters, we are going to explore some of the various roles and positions each of us will play in Christian ministry and we are going to see how they are much like the roles many of the Packers Hall of Fame players fulfilled when they played in Green Bay.

The difference is, of course, we are playing in the Super Bowl of Life, and the stakes are much higher than they were for the Packers. They could only win a trophy and be champions for a year. We can save souls from eternal destruction. The battle is fierce, but the rewards are eternal.

Once I had given the Lord my heart, I was His to use as He directed. I knew I wanted to play on His team, and it was time to learn what "plays we were going to run." It was time for me to learn what Iron-Man Christianity really was. I was on God's team now. I needed to understand His playbook. This is not optional, it is essential to winning.

[1]Many of the faithful men who taught me are still faithfully teaching these truths at that school. If you are interested in more information about it, see the Appendix in the back of this book.

Chapter Ten

First Things First:
Every Team has a Playbook

"Thy word is a lamp unto my feet,
and a light unto my path"
—Psalm 119:105

"Sanctify them in the truth; Your word is truth"
—John 17:17

Every team has a playbook. It is one of the first things you get from the team, even before you get a uniform. What is a playbook? The playbook is the coach's plan to win.

When Vince Lombardi was hired to coach at Green Bay, many coaches had already coached there. They each had their own playbook. Nobody expected Lombardi to use their playbook. Why? They had all lost! They needed a coach who could win!

Every team, every head coach has a playbook which contains what he believes is a winning strategy. Vince Lombardi was no different. Lombardi believed in a power running offense which would create strategic passing opportunities when the running plays were successful. Lombardi had learned much of the value of this strategy from his mentor Earl "Red" Blaik while coaching at

Army (West Point). He perfected his plan as the Offensive Coordinator for the New York Giants. When he got to Green Bay, he knew what he wanted to do. Now he needed to teach the players his game plan.

The "Game Plan"

The game plan is determined by the Coach, but it is often dictated by the opponent. What do we mean? The question for a coach every week is pretty simple. What do I need to do to prepare my team to win against this opponent? Each team you play will have certain strengths and certain weaknesses. They will do some things really well and others not so well. They will have some players who are extremely skilled and capable, but may have others who have serious, sometimes obvious, weaknesses.

The game plan is designed to expose and capitalize on the opponent's weaknesses and, at the same time, maximize your strengths and minimize your weaknesses. It is the job of the head coach and his staff to determine the best way to do this. It is their job to determine how their players *match up* against the opposing players at each position. Where do we have an advantage? Where do they have an advantage? How do they determine this?

They go to the "movies." What do they do at the movies? They study the enemy in action. They often spend endless hours watching game films of the opponent playing other teams. Why? It enables them to see what they do in certain situations. What are their strategies? What do they believe their strengths are? What weaknesses do they try to cover and protect? Are they correct in their assessments? What are their tendencies? What do they do in a "third down and long" situation? In a "third and short" situation? In whom do they have the most confidence? Who is their "go-to" guy in the most critical moments? To whom does the quarterback most often like to throw in these situations? All of these questions and many more are what the coaches are asking themselves each week.

At least that is what they are doing if they want to win! Once they see the "enemy strategy," they begin to design their own strategy and pick the plays they believe give them the best chance to win against the opposing team. This strategy is called "the game plan"; it is crafted and designed from the head coach's playbook.

The Bible Is God's Playbook

Every team has a playbook, and God's team is no different. The Bible is God's playbook. The Bible is not rocket science. You do not need a diploma or a degree in anything but diligence to understand it. God has given us His playbook and expects us to know it and study it, just like Lombardi would if we were playing for him. If we are teachable, He will be our Teacher. God has told us what He expects of us.

> "Be diligent to present yourself approved to God as a workman who does not need to be ashamed, handling accurately the word of truth." —2 Timothy 2:15 NASB

And how He will teach us:

> "...when He, the Spirit of truth comes, He will guide you into all the truth..." —John 16:13a

If we are going to be effective players on Christ's team we have to know the playbook, inside and out. We not only have to know our roles, we also have to understand the Coach's strategy and commit to it with a whole heart. We also have to know and understand where and under what conditions the game is going to be played. The truth is, this is not a game, it is a war. And you need to be aware that the conditions are not going to be favorable, and you will almost never have the *twelfth man* on your side. Who is the twelfth man?

The "Twelfth Man"

If you have been a football fan long, you will have heard the term the "twelfth man." It refers to the cheering fans in the stadium at a home game. Typically, the crowd at any given game will be heavily biased toward the home team (at least you hope so!) The energizing force that a loud, excited crowd can bring to a home game is very real. It can motivate and influence the home team to play beyond themselves; it can also make it almost impossible for the opposing team to function! It is like facing a team with twelve men instead of just eleven. *In Christianity there are no home games!* Might as well get used to it.

The game is played at "World-Forces Field," and it is controlled by the enemy. It is loud, noisy, and everything possible is done to make it difficult to win the game. It takes real discipline and mental toughness to keep our focus and filter out the noise and distractions the enemy will throw at us.

Some things you can't control, but there is one main point of attack you had better settle up front.

Do you believe the Bible is the Word of God? What authority does it have in your life? In your decisions? Do you let God guide your life through its principles? Or, is it just information?

"The Fool Has Said in His Heart...." —Psalm 14:1

We now live in a culture which has taught an entire generation of young people that *there is no God and, therefore, no authority to which we are accountable.* This has had ruinous effects on the lives and education of our young people.

All athletes understand both authority and accountability. Sports may be the last place where this is recognized. They are the keys to the unity which allows any team to succeed. If there is no respect for authority (that is, the head coach), then there is no way for him to command and direct the team to victory. It degenerates into a chaotic mess.

It is on the athletic field that we find the last remnant of the respect for authority which once made our educational system the envy of the world. It is no longer true in our classrooms. But the source of the problem is **not** primarily educational; it is moral.

Our massive public education cartel has determined that evolution, while it offers no answers to the ultimate questions about the meaning and purpose of life, is yet "settled science." Please pay close attention to this. There is no mistake about it: the primary impact the teaching of evolution has had on our young people is moral, not scientific. Nobody's life is really impacted by the idea that we were descended from a single-cell amoeba or monkeys or that the earth and civilization began with a "big bang." Unless you are a scientist, most people just do not care.

Diversionary Tactic?

The ongoing "creation vs. evolution" science debate, while important, may really be a diversion to the main enemy attack.

The real tragedy is the doubt about even the existence of God that is now embedded in the minds of a generation of young people. That has been catastrophic! It is not that these young people actively disbelieve in God, they just do not see why He matters. Their professors have dismissed the idea of God as unscientific and, therefore, irrelevant, so they do, too. In effect, God is obsolete, a crutch we no longer need.

Fact: If mainstream Darwinian evolution is true, that it all started with a chance "big bang," then there is no God. It is the unavoidable conclusion of the teaching of Darwinian evolution.

Fact: If evolution is true, then the Bible cannot be true. Darwinian evolution and the Bible *cannot* both be true. Let me repeat that. They cannot both be true. There is no middle ground on which to stand.

The repercussions of this are enormous. We are seeing in it the impact on our culture over the last generation. But the results were inevitable. If evolution is true and there is no God, then there is no "Law of God" to disobey, and therefore, there is no accountability for sin because there is no one to whom to be morally accountable. There is obviously no Savior and no salvation since there is nothing from which to be saved. There cannot be any wrath of God to flee from if there is no God.

The Bible says that those who believe this are fools. Psalm 14:1 says, "The fool has said in his heart, there is no God." Either this is true or it is false. You have to decide if you believe the Bible is God's Word. You have to decide if what the Bible teaches is absolute truth or not. There is no middle ground on this.

To put it another way, you have to decide whether you believe

Genesis 1 and John 1 are truth based in reality or just stories meant to encourage you. If you do not believe, without reservation, that God created the heavens and the earth, then the Bible has no more to say to you.

Everything in life depends on whether God exists and what He says is true. Without that concrete foundation, you will be building your foundation on sand. Eventually it will collapse. To put it in football terms, if you cannot believe in what the coach says, you need to be playing for another team, one with a coach you can trust wholeheartedly.

To follow our football analogy, if you have doubts about the strategy the coaches have designed to win the game, what is going to happen in the fourth quarter when the pressure is on and the game is on the line and a hostile crowd is making it almost impossible to run your plays? It is too late to try to re-think the strategy. The doubts will cripple you, your decisions will be tentative, and the potential for the team to win the game will likely be lost to mistakes.

This is why the first priority in your life has to be to know the Lord, intimately, as a person. The second priority is to know His Word and believe it is truth you can rely on. Do you believe this verse?

> "All Scripture is inspired by God (literally 'God-breathed') and profitable for teaching, for reproof, for correction, for instruction in righteousness; that the man of God may be adequate, equipped for every good work."
>
> —2 Timothy 3:16-17

Either it is true or it is false. If God does not exist, then this verse has to be false. If He exists, this verse says He is the *source* of all Bible truth and its purpose is to equip us to do our job, to fulfill our role in His "game plan."

You have to have it settled in your heart that you know the Lord is real, that He is the Son of God who loved you and gave Himself for you. You have to know in your heart that the man or the woman who does not believe this is the fool, not you.

And please remember, God has said to love that fool. You also were once that fool. Remember also that the fool is blinded by the god of this world into this foolish thinking, just as you once were. It is your job to love that fool and to be the light of God in his life. There is a practical reality you always need to keep in mind. The great evangelist, D.L. Moody summed it up well:

> "One in 100 men will read the Bible. The other 99 will read the Christian. You may be the only 'Bible' some people ever see."

Once you have settled the issue as to whether you are willing to play by God's playbook, then it is time to learn how His system works. Who is in charge? Who calls the plays on God's team? How do the plays in the playbook get called and executed in the game?

Bart Starr had to learn Lombardi's system. He struggled for a while, but once he had mastered it, the game changed for him and he became Lombardi's voice on the field. It also enabled him to end up in the NFL Hall of Fame. But things did not look very promising at the beginning.

Chapter Eleven

The Iron-Man Quarterback:
The Coach on the Field

**"A holy life will produce the deepest impression.
Lighthouses blow no horns, they only shine."
—Dwight L. Moody**

S omething always went wrong! That could easily be the way Green Bay Packers Hall of Fame quarterback Bart Starr would sum up his first three years in the NFL. Some actually thought he was just a "screw-up." Many were convinced he did not have the skills to play in the NFL. He was not highly regarded. The truth is, he really did not have great skills.

But what else could you expect from a quarterback who was drafted in the 17th round of the NFL draft! To give you some perspective on that, Starr's Hall of Fame right tackle, Forrest Gregg, was drafted in the 2nd round (20th overall), Starr was the 200th player drafted that year! When Starr first reported to training camp his rookie year, they gave him the number #42. Why was that? They thought the only chance he had to make the team was as a *defensive* back. It was not an auspicious beginning, and it did not get much better for several years. But he did end up in the NFL Hall of Fame! What changed? How did that happen?

Though Starr did not have a strong arm or quick feet, he did have something that greatly endeared him to Coach Lombardi. He was a diligent student, he wanted to learn everything that Lombardi wanted to teach him. Starr was a great learner and Lombardi was a great teacher! That is a great combination. Why do we care?

The quarterback (QB) is the coach on the field. He is going to guide the team in executing the strategy the head coach has designed to win the game. We are all going to have quarterbacks in our lives. At different times and in different ways, the Lord is going to use them to lead us, guide us, shepherd us, motivate us, and when necessary, correct us as we travel the path of following Christ. As we learn and mature, we may become the QB in the lives of others, performing the same role. The analogy is not perfect, but it is too strong to miss. As Christians we often get to choose our QB, so we better choose carefully. Our QB needs to be an Iron-Man.

What Makes a Good Iron-Man Quarterback?

There will be different ideas on this, but I think at a minimum he has to have at least these four characteristics.

First, he has to be able to lead. True leadership requires character. Other people must be able to see something in him which will cause them to want to follow his lead as the quarterback. As we will see, this has much to do with the character and decisions others see him make.

Second, he has to inspire confidence. This is the "belief" factor. The team has to believe that the QB knows how to win.

This is a function of knowledge, preparation, and results. Confidence grows as success is achieved.

Third, he has to have at least some skills. He may not be extraordinary in what he does, but he does have to be competent and consistent in the skills he does have. Some skills are gifts, others can be learned and enhanced with practice.

Fourth, he has to be mentally tough. This is crucial; without it he will fold under pressure. There will be constant efforts to break his concentration, confuse him, or distract him from the main objective. He must be able to defend against these and, more important, he must be able to recover quickly.

Bart Starr Was an Iron-Man Quarterback. Why?

First, it was because he had *character*. He lived by biblical principles. His teammates knew that and respected him for it, even though many of them did not embrace those same principles. They knew he was solid, dependable. In the early years of his career he faced real adversity, but his teammates saw that he never gave up. When it was his time to lead, they were willing to follow him. He had proven character.

Second, he had *confidence*. Starr had allowed Lombardi to teach him and teach him and teach him. Some said "Starr was Lombardi's creation," and Starr readily agreed and considered it a great compliment.

What gave him confidence? Diligent preparation. By the time the game rolled around every weekend and the game plan was decided, Starr believed he was prepared for every potential defense the opposing team would use to try to stop the Packers, and that they had the answer to overcome it.

If they executed their game plan properly, Starr believed they would win. And he was able to communicate this confidence to his team. They came to believe that if everyone executed his assignment properly, they could score a touchdown on every play. As they began to win games, their confidence in Starr (and themselves) continued to grow. This is how they became a dynasty.

Third, while by no means without skills, Starr did not have superior skills. Though he did not have the greatest arm strength, what he did have was tremendous accuracy. He led the NFL in passing completion percentage three times. He retired with the highest completion percentage of any QB up to that time. His mental skills kept him ahead of the opposing team. When they made adjustments, he knew exactly what to do to counter those adjustments. He was in control, and his team knew it. That leads to the last point.

Fourth, Starr was *mentally tough*. He will be the first to admit that he was not mentally tough when he started. He was affected too much by his emotions. Emotions can be powerful motivators. You need emotions to be an athlete and compete at the highest levels. But you need to be able to control those emotions or they will control you. If that happens, your concentration and focus are broken, and the pressure will cause you to make mistakes, mistakes that usually end up causing you to lose the game.

How does all this apply to us? Assuming we are wise enough to recognize that we need godly leadership in our lives, God will give us godly *Iron-Men* to act as our quarterback. He will be our "coach on the field," guiding us so that we are able to avoid many of the pitfalls we will face in life and stay on the path of following Christ. No godly leader claims to know it all. He would be too wise to do something so foolish.

At different times and stages in life we may have a new QB from whom we can learn new things. But the attributes of a true Iron-Man leader are the same for all and often mirror those of a good NFL quarterback. But by far the key quality of an Iron-Man is character.

What Are the Essentials of Iron-Man Character?

In deciding whom you will follow in life, the first characteristic you should look for is Character. Does he or she have strong character? Biblically strong character?

Character is the fruit of Principles, Discipline, and Decisions. We need to look at each of these.

"Principles" are the standards you live by. They clarify and declare right and wrong in your life. They are the rules, the guardrails that keep you on the right path. Where do these come from? How do you decide? Are they something you have thought through or just something someone else told you was right? How do you know if they are right? Is it just a matter of what you feel is right at the moment?

Most of us inherit our principles, at least at the beginning. They are just part of our upbringing. We are raised to believe that certain things are right and others are wrong. There is nothing wrong with this, as long as these principles are based on truth. There is only one source of absolute truth: God's Word. So you need to be certain your guiding life principles are biblically-based. If they are not, you need to make adjustments so that they are.

Next is "Discipline." Discipline is not just about the direction you are going; it is about the limits you impose on yourself that will allow you to focus on the goal you want to reach. Jim Rohn says it this way, "Discipline is the bridge between goals and accomplishments."

Vince Lombardi said it this way, "It's easy to have faith and discipline when you're winning, when you're number one. What you've got to have is faith and discipline when you're not a winner."

In his mind, this is the only way you could become a winner. Along with Principles and Discipline, remember this:

Decisions, Not Desire, Will Determine Your Destiny.

It is what is often called the "Principle of the Path." I do not know whether this idea is original with mega-church Pastor Andy Stanley or not, but he is dead-on right about it. Any path you choose to go down will have an end, a destination. Once you start down that path you cannot escape its destiny. As long as you stay on the path you will reach your goal.

But it takes real discipline to stay on the path. It also takes real wisdom and discipline to realize you are on the wrong path, and to get off—and stay off!

Principles and discipline lead to good decisions. You will be constantly faced with temptations and not all of them will be bad or evil. Sometimes good can be the enemy of the best. God's plan always has the best as the goal for your life, though it may not seem like it at first sometimes.

An Iron-Man leader will always encourage you to go down the path that leads to your being the best you can be for God. He will teach you biblical principles which will form a foundation for right and wrong which will lead to a life lived for His honor and glory. This destiny is certain.

Chapter Twelve

Confidence, Competence, and Toughness

"There are no secrets to success. It is the result of preparation, hard work, and learning from failure."　　　　—General Colin Powell

"A winning effort begins with preparation."
　　　　　　　　　　—Coach Joe Gibbs

Confidence: Inspiring Leadership

Once you have determined that the one you are following has solid, biblically-based character, there are three other qualities to look for: confidence, competence and mental toughness.

An Iron-Man leader will not only have good character and the ability to lead his people, he will inspire confidence in them. They will want to follow him. Let's inject a note of caution here. There is an important difference between inspired leadership and inspiring leadership.

Inspired leadership is sometimes just a mask for arrogance. Arrogance and boastfulness are not the same as confidence. Arrogance is usually the fruit of someone who is highly or uniquely-gifted in some area, and who thinks he or she is infinitely better than all the other "players" on the field. For example, some people are very gifted speakers. They can keep a crowd spellbound, amazed at their gifts and talents. They can persuade people to follow them, convincing them that they will be better off if they do. Too often, this is not inspiration, it is actually manipulation. Natural gifts, temperament, and personality can be helpful to anyone. But they are no substitute for godly character, spiritual power, and discipline.

The truly godly leader not only inspires people to follow him, he inspires confidence in them to do what God calls them to do. He encourages them not only to be ready to do whatever God calls them to do, he shows them why they should believe they can. On what is that confidence built?

*　　*　　*　　*　　*

Confidence is the knowledge that you are prepared and have the spiritual resources to meet every situation you are likely to face in your current circumstances. *True confidence is the fruit of diligent study and preparation; it leads to the kind of faith and self-confidence that can stand firm in any situation.* The secret to Bart Starr's great success was not his great skills, it was his preparation! It was the foundation of his confidence.

Like Starr, the Iron-Man leader will be diligent in his preparation. He will sit side-by-side with the head coach to craft the game plan for the next week. When they are done, they will be of "one mind" and the team should be able to sense the presence of the Head Coach (Jesus Christ) in the midst as His truth is proclaimed by the godly leader. He will give you food for the mind, the soul and the spirit. It will inspire confidence in the hearers that if they are willing to follow, they will succeed.

How are you going to recognize a truly godly Iron-Man leader? Here is a good test. Find out who and what he is committed to.

*   *   *   *   *

One thing that always impressed those 1958 Packers was the growing knowledge that everything Lombardi was doing, even the things they thought were insanely difficult, were designed to enable them to win games. He literally gave himself for them, many times working 18-hour days, just to make it possible for them to win! And they knew it. It inspired them to give themselves wholeheartedly to his mission.

Many nights the quarterback was right alongside the coach. They were so united in the "game plan" that having Bart Starr in the huddle was just like having Lombardi there! Interestingly, in the end, many of the players acknowledged that the longer they followed him, what they wanted more than anything was not primarily to win, but to please Lombardi and gain his approval. This is what Bart Starr wanted most. Winning became a by-product of their devotion and service to the coach. Think about that.

This should be the Iron-Man leader's motivation as well. He is, quite literally, intended to be an extension of Christ into the lives of those he leads. He labors diligently to care for the sheep under his charge, not only because he cares about the sheep, but also because he desires to hear his Head Coach say one day, "Well done, good and faithful servant." The sheep will recognize the shepherd's true motivation. They will know if you are serving the Lord or yourself.

You will know you are succeeding when you see these young disciples living for the Lord and desiring His approval more than anything else in their lives.

The Iron-Man leader must lead and inspire confidence in those he leads. His diligent preparation and care must inspire the belief that they are prepared to win the battles they will face in life. Each disciple under his charge needs to be adequately-equipped and nurtured into spiritual maturity. In order to do this the godly leader will need at least basic skills in knowledge and communication. It has been well said, "You can't lead someone where you have not already gone yourself."

Competence: Solid "Fundamentals"

Having the "basic skills" or "fundamentals" to fulfill the role of QB in another's life does not mean you have to be a biblical scholar. You could highlight many areas which would be helpful in the role of godly leadership, but two crucial traits would have to include these: diligence and faithfulness.

When the apostle Paul instructed Timothy about setting up the leadership roles in the early church, this is what he told him to do: "The things which you have heard from me...entrust these to faithful men who will be able to teach others also..." (2Timothy 2:2).

Of course, he needs to know and master the basic truths of Scripture and be able to teach them to those he leads. But to do this only requires that he be diligent in his study and trust the

Lord for the illumination and enablement of the Holy Spirit, and be faithful in the execution of his duties.

*   *   *   *   *

Today we are often kept spellbound by the "professionally-choreographed," media-driven church services. Many pastors feel that the mega-church is the ultimate measure of success. This is not surprising since we live in a culture which measures success by numbers and ratings. We should not try to deceive ourselves about this; it is very difficult to escape. But that does not make it right or, in any biblical way, a true measure of success.

The Bible is very clear on this. Jesus makes a solemn point (that every mega-church pastor should consider carefully) when He says, "Enter by the narrow gate; for the gate is wide, and the way is broad that leads to destruction, and many are those who enter by it. For the gate is small, and the way is narrow that leads to life, and few are those who find it" (Matthew 7:13-14). Huge numbers are not a trustworthy barometer of spiritual success, it is often not a good sign at all.

In trying to reconcile all this and discern whether you are following a true Iron-Man leader, an important question to ask might be this: Would this leader still do everything the same if his church or study group only had 10, 20, or 50 people rather than 500, 1000, or 10,000? This puts the spotlight on the real question, namely, am I doing this work to honor the Lord or so that I can appear "successful"?

Another question would be this: Is the Lord "adding to their number" or is the church multiplying because it offers "state-of-the-art" worship services and "country club" amenities for virtually no cost? To those who think they can preach the gospel of Jesus Christ and not offend people, I would only remind them of the words of the Lord of the true gospel. In John 15:18, 20, Jesus says:

> "If the world hates you, you know that it has hated Me
> before it hated you. Remember the word that I said to
> you, 'a slave is not greater than his master.' If they
> persecuted Me, they will also persecute you...."

This is not to say that there are not godly, faithful men of God pastoring large churches; there are. But the more the appearance of worldly/financial success surrounds you, the more the pressure will build to maintain that "success," even if it means using the world's methods.

It is a difficult and often precarious balance. Many have fallen trying to navigate that path. The bottom line is that the true gospel is not a "deal" too good to pass up. According to the Bible, "many are called, but few are chosen;" "few" find the narrow path to life and follow it (see Matthew 22:14). Why is this? Because, as we have seen, to follow Christ means to take up a cross and live for Him. You cannot serve two masters. You cannot go on living for yourself and live for Him at the same time. You cannot play by the world's playbook and win Christ. You have to choose.

I am constantly receiving postcards in the mail touting the newest mega-church in the area, some promising me free coffee and the ultimate answers for happiness in my life. It sounds like the chance of a lifetime. How could I pass it up? What I often find is, these churches are using what I call an *entertainment model* for church growth. What is that?

The goal of all entertainment (sports included) is to get you to come see the performance (as a fan or spectator) and go away satisfied with the performance, deceived into thinking you actually participated or your life was changed by it. The truth is, you simply got what you paid for. What? Free entertainment. This method is almost always very successful in drawing large numbers of people. The question is: Are they being genuinely born again or just entertained?

The Iron-Man leader will accept nothing less than a life lived for God's glory. It is his job to stay diligent and faithful in caring for the Lord's people, teaching and training them until they become Iron-Man Christians. These are just the basic skills. Ultimately, his goal is to prepare those under his care and guidance to work together as a body, as a team, as a single unit. In order to do this successfully, they are going to need one more thing to succeed. They are going to need to be tough.

Mental Toughness

Lastly, the Iron-Man leader must have mental toughness. Bart Starr said one of the greatest things that Lombardi did for him was instill mental toughness. He could never have succeeded without it. He freely admits that he did not have it when he came to Green Bay. This is an often overlooked attribute in the Christian life.

It is critically important for every Christian to be mentally tough, especially in these days of terrible moral decline and shallow, self-pleasing, and often false teaching.

What is mental toughness? It can be described several ways. Bart Starr talked about it as the "fire in the belly" that drives a person to win, overcoming all obstacles, the attitude that thinks finishing second equals finishing last.

Having said that, it is important to understand that mentally tough people who finish second do not see finishing second as a failure, as Lombardi would say, as long as they played with all their heart. To them, finishing second becomes motivation. They see how close they came to winning and they are motivated to strive harder. If the truth be told, Lombardi rarely thought he lost a game, he just ran out of time. Eventually, he would have won! This is clearly a winner's mindset. If anyone should have a winner's mindset, it is the Christian. He knows how the game ends!

But mental toughness has other aspects which are crucial to our faith-walk on this earth. It also means that we are not easily distracted from our goal. And even when we are, we are able to rebound quickly and get back on track.

Distractions that break our focus and concentration come in all forms. The most common are emotional distractions, things which cause us to become angry, frustrated, disappointed, or depressed. It is mental toughness which enables us to recover quickly and reduce these to minor distractions.

Tiger Woods is universally recognized as one of the most intensely focused, mentally tough athletes in the world today. Obviously, he has had serious off-field, personal failures in his life. But from his earliest days, his father trained him to be mentally tough. One of the most famous techniques he used was to drop Tiger's golf bag (with all the clubs in it!) in the middle of his back swing. It would cause a total break in his concentration. But over time He learned to forget it and refocus quickly. He knew this would make Tiger mentally tough under pressure. He was right.

Mental toughness comes from facing tough circumstances, overcoming them, and continuing to perform at a high level. As Christians, as followers of Christ, we need to be mentally tough, able to recover quickly from mistakes, distractions, disappointments, even sin. When repentance is needed, we need to repent, receive God's forgiveness, and refocus on the mission He has given us, not wallow in self-pity.

Is all this biblical? Listen to the apostle Paul. If there was ever a man who was mentally tough, it was Paul!

To the Philippians: "...this one thing I do, forgetting what lies behind, I press on..." (Philippians 3:13b).

To Timothy: "Endure hardship with me, as a good soldier of Jesus Christ" (2 Timothy 2:3).

It takes mental toughness to suffer hardship and stay the course. It is the job of the Iron-Man leader to train his people to be mentally tough, with their eyes "fixed on Jesus." There is no way to finish the race or accomplish God's mission if we are always looking back or looking inward, much less standing still. Remember:

The goal line is always in front of you, never behind you.

David Livingstone, God's missionary to Africa, put it this way:

"I will go anywhere...as long as it is forward."

That is the way an Iron-Man thinks.

Chapter Thirteen

Iron-Man Offense:
The Plan to Score and Win

"If the goal is not to win, why do they keep score?"

—Vince Lombardi

T he goal of every team is to win the game. Offense includes all the tools, weapons, resources, and skills we can use to achieve victory over our opponent. The Iron-Man Christian has to be confident, skilled and mentally tough. When we organize these weapons and resources into a planned strategy, we would call it an "offensive strategy" for victory. Again, it is not a perfect analogy to the Packers "offensive strategy," but many of the principles of God's strategy are the same.

Green Bay's Offensive Strategy: The "Power Sweep"

Many would say that the Packers really had only one offensive play. In a sense, that was true. They called it the Green Bay "power sweep." You would think that if this were true, it would be very easy to stop it. The same play could not possibly work over and over. After all, if the defense knows what is coming, it will simply anticipate it and be there to stop it before it ever starts. At least, that is what you would think.

Have you ever tried to step on a roach? Most of us have. When you start to go one way, he goes the other! The fact is, he can go in any direction. Where he goes is purely dependent on where you go. His goal is simple: to avoid you. That was the secret of Green Bay's "power sweep."

It may look like just one play, but it was possible to create more than a dozen different options and they all depended on how the defense reacted. If you went one way, they went the other. The critical thing was that this was done "on the fly," with the pulling guards and tackles leading the way. The halfback or the fullback would follow their lead and sense which way the blockers were pushing the defense and either go with the opening or cut back along the seam to an open lane.

Of course, it helped to have Hall of Famers like Jim Ringo and Forrest Gregg blocking for you. Not to mention Jerry Kramer! [How is it possible that the one guard named to the NFL's 50th anniversary and All-Decade teams for the 1960's, a 6-time All-Pro is not in the Hall of Fame! Something seems terribly wrong in the system here.]

It also helped to have Hall of Famers Paul Hornung and Jim Taylor running behind them. But you should remember that all of these future greats were also on the team the year before when they went 1-10-1. Their greatness was only potential. Hornung was so depressed over his own struggles, he almost quit the team. It was not until Lombardi took control of the team and the players embraced his strategy (and paid the price to master it) that the Packers began to win. And they kept on winning!

The Green Bay "power sweep" was their primary weapon. What is the Iron-Man Christian's primary offensive weapon?

The Christian's Primary Offensive Weapon: A Transformed Life

The Christian's most effective offensive weapon is, like Green Bay, really simple: our primary weapon is Jesus Christ. Christ in me (by His Spirit) transforming me and Christ through me so that others may see Him. The apostle John summed it up in John 1:4. He said, "In Him was life and the life was the light of men." It is His power and authority; it is His love, His salvation, and His victory that we proclaim. That is the winning play. No other play will work.

That Life and Light is now in me. He leads us from victory to victory in the train of His triumph. It is Christ in us that is the certain hope of glory. It is Christ through us that allows that light to be seen by others so that they can be drawn to Him and share that glory as well. It is when the transformed life is visibly seen by those around us that it simply cannot be denied.

But in order to maintain the victory, we have to maintain an intimate communion, walking in close fellowship with the Lord. Paul describes it as being one with Him; John calls it abiding in Christ. You have the mind of Christ in the Scriptures; this is God's playbook. This is the foundation of truth that God's game plan is built around. But you have to be personally ready when He calls. You have to be in a place where you can "hear His voice." You have to know what "play" He wants to call now and what your "assignment" is on that play. How do you do this? Like any other relationship, it takes knowledge, preparation, and constant communication. Prayer and worship are how the Christian maintains this intimate relationship with God. This is how you "keep your head in the game" for God.

Are You Prepared to Play?

In order to be prepared to play and win on Sunday, the Packers spent at least 10 times as much time in practice and preparation, both individually and as a team. That statement is not an exaggeration; in fact, they probably spent more than 30 hours preparing to play a three-hour game. Their personal preparation was just as important as their team "prep." The same is true of the Christian. He must work diligently to be ready to play at the highest level at all times.

The early church knew what their job was. They were to preach "the gospel of the Kingdom" and share the good news that Jesus Christ, their King, had died for their sins and risen from the dead. Because it was now possible for all men's sins to be forgiven, they urged them to repent of their sins, abandon their futile way of life and follow Christ. The New Testament message of the Kingdom of God and the Risen Christ literally transformed the world.

In their ministry of making disciples, they faced challenges, both internal and external. Acts 6 reveals the response of the apostles to certain distractions and crystallized what they deemed as essential to their ministry. In Acts 6:5 the apostle Peter highlights two things: prayer and the ministry of the Word. These are the two essentials which must be mastered and protected if we are to be ready to "play" on God's team.

The obvious question is why? Beware, especially if you have grown up in the church environment, of thinking you already know the answer. Knowing the answer is one thing; living the answer is quite another. We have to be truly committed to succeed in God's mission. The cost can sometimes be quite high. Since these are the keys to a transformed life and our effectiveness for Christ, let's look at them more closely.

Prayer and "the Word"

What is so special about this "team"? Prayer and "the Word" are both continually talked about in the New Testament. The apostle John is particularly fond of them. The reason is that they describe the basic elements of our relationship with God; it is a two-way street.

Prayer is how man speaks to God; *the Word* is how God speaks to man. This is the way God has designed it. This is what enables God to fulfill His purposes in and through us. This is how we will be able to know and do His will. The Bible is God's playbook. We can learn a great deal about how we should treat it from the Packers' experience.

Mastering God's Playbook

Every Packers player had to know and learn the team's playbook. This was **not** optional. They would be dismissed from the team if they refused to master it. It was essential. There was no substitute for it. Why? They would be useless to the coach without it. Why? <u>Because it was the main tool the coach would use to communicate with his players.</u>

The playbook is what they would use, week after week, to design the winning strategy they would use to overcome their next opponent. It was the common link, the common language between the coach and the team. Everything they shared was built around that book. It gave the team the ability to marshal their offensive forces and enable them to act in unity. When the coach called a particular play, they would all know the play, know their assignment, and what they were trying to accomplish with it. To the Packers, it was like "a divine directive" on that play.

Again, take note of this! *Once the playbook was mastered, that was not the end; it was only the beginning of their communication!* It was what made strategic communication possible—during the game! It was what allowed the players to understand what the coach wanted to do. This is what allowed them to function as a single unit. From this point on, the coach and the players could speak the same language, they were on the same page, they knew the "endgame," they could begin to function as a team to accomplish the goal—and win the game.

Hopefully, by now, the analogy is clear. Mastering the Word of God is what enables us to know the overall plan of God. We need to know God, personally and intimately. We need to know the truths of God's Word so well that they are like second nature to us. We have to be committed to living by them, just as the Packers were committed to playing by Lombardi's playbook. This is all just preparation to get us ready for the real task which is walking in the Holy Spirit and bringing the light of the gospel to lost men and women wherever God calls us to "play" for Him.

Prayer is essential to us. It is like being in the huddle with the coach himself. It is where His strategy for a particular play is revealed. Prayer is fundamental to the Christian's life with God. Without it, we lose the ability to hear the Coach's voice. To follow our analogy, it is like we know there is a game going on, but we are basically just spectators, sitting on the sidelines. We want the team to win, but we are clueless about what play is being called or whether the coach wants us to do anything. Can you imagine what Lombardi would say to a player like this? He would say, "Get your head in the game!" Prayer is how we keep our head in the game with God. Since this is so crucial, let's make sure we have the "fundamentals" of prayer right.

Chapter Fourteen

Prayer: The Fundamentals

"Prayer does not fit us for the greater work,
prayer is the greater work."

—Oswald Chambers

Prayer is the constant privilege of the Christian to talk to "the Coach." It is our lifeline to the source of all life. God is omniscient, omnipresent, and available 24/7. The Bible tells us He is never weary of our coming to Him. Whenever we fail or face disappointments or are discouraged about some situation, He is there to comfort and to commune. He knows the challenges we face, and He has the answers we need.

Having said that, it is also essential that we have our priorities right in prayer. For far too many people, prayer is a last resort. It is where we come when we find ourselves in a crisis, with no other resources. It would be laughable, if it were not so sad. Think about it.

What we are really saying is, "Well, we have tried everything else...and we have no answer. Let's pray, let's see if the omnipotent, eternal God who created the heavens and the earth, who raised Jesus from the dead...let's see if He might possibly have an answer." Would it not make a lot more sense to seek Him first? How do we miss this? Sometimes common sense is not very common.

What are we disturbed about? What are we discouraged about? Is the problem or the mess we are in because we are engaged in accomplishing His mission or one we decided to pursue on our own? Are we attempting this in our strength or His? These are important questions.

In Luke 11 the disciples came to Jesus and said, "Lord, teach us to pray." The Lord kept to the same playbook He used in Matthew 6. Note this: He taught them from the playbook He used for Himself! He taught them the fundamentals, the three governing principles of prayer:

1. Prayer always begins with God: "Hallowed be Thy Name" (exalting Him as holy, reverently fearing Him).

2. Prayer has one primary concern, namely, God's glory: "Thy Kingdom Come" (saved souls are transferred to the Kingdom of God).

3. Prayer has one primary mission: "Thy Will be done on earth" (the establishing of God's Kingdom in the hearts of men is the primary goal of God).

What do you not see first? Prayer for me and my needs! Does God not care about my needs? Of course He does, but it is in the next part of the prayer. He already knows what you need anyway—and He has made provision for it. "For this reason I say to you, do not be worried about your life, as to what you will eat or what you will drink; nor for your body, as to what you will put on" (Matthew 6:25).

The Lord says exactly that in the same chapter, "...your heavenly Father knows that you need all these things. But seek first His kingdom and His righteousness, and all these things will be added to you" (Matthew 6:32b-33).

What do these fundamentals reveal should be our primary focus and purpose in prayer? To seek first God's kingdom (Matthew 6:33). If you do that, God has promised to take care of all your earthly needs. Why does He do this? So that we will be free to focus on God's game plan, to serve Him in the real mission of life, the mission of Christ—to seek and to save those who are lost! But we need more than discipline and dedication for that; we need power, divine power.

Prayer and the Holy Spirit

Prayer (with all its derivatives—pray, prayed, etc.) are mentioned over 125 times in the New Testament. It comes in many forms, the most common is as a petition, a plea for God to do something or cause something to happen. This is entirely biblical. Paul writes to the Philippians, "Be anxious for nothing, but in everything by prayer and supplication with thanksgiving let your requests be made known to God" (Philippians 4:6).

God knows what we need to fulfill His purpose in our life. Prayer is His way of letting us in on the fulfillment of that need. It also helps to constantly remind us of who alone is the source of that fulfillment, namely, God Himself.

But to pray effectively and see things happen requires more

than just general instructions. Too many Christians want to use prayer to get what we want rather than letting God use our prayers to get what He wants. To get it right, we need to be willing to do His will in everything. But even being willing does not make us able. That is why God gave us the gift of the Holy Spirit.

Author A.W. Pink once famously wrote, "We can no more pray without the Holy Spirit than we can create a world." We would never be foolish enough to think we could create a world. But few would hesitate to pray—anytime, anywhere. What is Pink's point? He is saying that only God truly knows the mind of God and, since the Holy Spirit is God, He alone can lead us into the knowledge of the will of God and (when our prayers fall short of His will) He can and will intercede for us. Many times the desire of our hearts is right even if our petitions are not exactly aligned with His perfect solution.

For example, many dear brothers and sisters believe and pray for God's glory to be manifested in the healing of a particular person's affliction. They truly want the glory of God. Many also believe that it is God's will for us *always* to be healed, that is, if those who are praying, pray in faith. Of course, many times the person is not healed. Unfairly, the deficiency is laid at the feet of those who obviously did not sufficiently believe for the healing, including the afflicted persons themselves. But was that prayer accurate? Biblically accurate? Did God not answer those prayers? I want to make two points here. This is not merely an academic issue. Sadly it is an all too common experience.

Understanding the Place of Faith in the Power of Prayer

First is the issue of faith. Faith, biblically, is what we know of as trust. We exercise true faith when we entrust something precious to us to another. A simple illustration would be depositing our paycheck into our bank account. Some of us do it personally, but some companies direct-deposit our paychecks into our bank account. We expect to live, eat, pay our bills, etc. with our paycheck. We have earned that money with our personal labor. It is very important to us.

We have trusted our employer to pay us what they owe, on time, each week. We have also trusted them to give us our check personally or to directly deposit our paycheck into our bank account. We then trust our bank to have that money available for us as we need it. If the bank goes bankrupt because they have invested our money in risky ventures they will have violated our trust.

Think about this. Will my believing or trusting harder make my money any more secure? No. **The power of my faith is in the object of my faith.** If my bank managers have the character and integrity they should have and act responsibly, my faith will be rewarded and my money safe and secure. If it does not, then my trying to believe harder will not change a thing.

The same is true of faith in God. The power of the faith is in the object of the faith: that is, God Himself. The question is not whether I believe or trust Him hard enough, it is whether I trust Him at all–and that I continue to trust Him! As an example, if I am praying to God for the healing of a dear friend, the very fact that I come to Him and not someone else is evidence that my faith is real. The fact that God did not respond the way I desired does not mean that I did not trust God or that God did not answer my prayer! How can that be?

What is Our Real Purpose in Prayer?

Was not the fundamental desire of our prayer that God would be glorified? Of course it was, at least it should have been. I have lived long enough now to see that God is often more glorified when His choice men and women are allowed to suffer afflictions (sometimes terribly difficult afflictions), but they find His sustaining grace enables them to not just survive the difficulty, but thrive in it! It is humbling to watch these dear saints overcome sometimes incredible challenges.

God may not answer the way we would have liked, but in His eternal wisdom our prayers were answered in ways we would not likely choose, but in ways that glorified Him more than we could have thought. This is why the Holy Spirit is so essential in prayer.

The goal of prayer cannot be just to bring a laundry list of petitions hoping God will answer some of them. The goal of prayer is to bring the power and authority of the eternal God into a circumstance—either to make it right or make it different.

But this can only happen if our prayer is according to the will of God. Our prayers cannot change God or God's will. If we think about it, we would not want it any other way. If God is perfect in every way, gracious, kind, loving and forgiving, we should not want to change His will. If Paul is correct in what he says in Romans 12:2 that the will of God is "good and acceptable and perfect," then we should want to know what His will is and pray for that!

But many times we do not know what the will of God is. That

is why we have the Holy Spirit of God dwelling in us; He intercedes for the saints according to the will of God (Romans 8:26-27).

When we can pray according to the will of God, we can be assured our prayers will be answered. They may or may not always be answered the way we would like them answered, but if our hearts are truly aligned with His heart, then we can be assured His answer will be good, acceptable and perfect. They will be answered in His perfect time and in a way that glorifies God the most, and that should be the dominant desire of our hearts. It should also give us peace.

The process begins with a solid understanding of the truths of the Bible. Your goal must be to master these truths. Then, with that foundation, your prayers should seek to glorify Him by seeking the revelation of His perfect will in every circumstance you face. This requires the spiritual sensitivity which only "walking by the Spirit" can give.

The real question is, how can we get to the place where our hearts are "one" with God's? How do we "tune" our hearts so that we are "one spirit with the Lord"? There is a way, but for many it is a lost art. As the world has bludgeoned its way into the church, we have lost or forgotten the supreme importance of worshipping God. One wonders whether we even know what it is anymore. What we do know is that without true worship, the foundation for a winning strategy in the spiritual battles of life is missing.

Worship is as essential to believing prayer as repentance is to salvation. One simply does not happen without the other. In reminding ourselves of the necessity of true worship, we may also "step on some toes" as we highlight some modern misconceptions of what worship is. The trend seems to be that the louder our worship gets the more God-honoring it is. Where is that in the Bible? Praise is at the core of our worship, to be sure, and praise can take many forms. But when our so-called worship rises to rock concert, ear-splitting levels, we seriously wonder if this is what God means when we read, "I will sing to the LORD as long as I live; I will sing praise to my God while I have my being" (Psalm 104:33).

Such praise requires us to be able to think as well as sing. There has to be a place for verses like these also....

> "There will be silence before You, and praise in Zion, O God.... O You who hear prayer, to You all men come."
>
> —Psalm 65:1-2

> "God is spirit and those who worship Him must worship in spirit and truth." —John 4:24

Since it is so essential, let's think about what worship really is.

Chapter Fifteen

Worship:
The Believer's Response to
God's Greatness

"Worship is a response to greatness. A man does not become a worshipper merely by saying, "Now I shall become a worshipper." That is impossible. That cannot be done. A man becomes a worshipper when he sees something great that calls forth his admiration or his worship. That is the only way worshippers are made. Worship answers to greatness."
                                    —Pastor Tom Wells

I think this quote captures something of the essence of true worship. Worship is our response to *greatness*. We know greatness when we see it. We respond to greatness when we see it. We see this all the time in the sports and entertainment worlds. What can we conclude from this? When people do not worship someone, we know that it is not because they can't, it is because they do not see greatness.

When a person is able to perform at an unusually high level, they will attract fans (fanatics). Why? People respond to what they perceive as greatness with outpourings of appreciation, praise, and, glory. We see it all the time. For over a decade one of the most successful TV shows was called *American Idol.* They did not call it that by accident. They knew exactly what their goal was: to create an American Idol with millions of adoring fans to buy their music and come to their concerts. Call it by any name you want, including idolatry, but this is worship. You can argue about the quality or true value of its "greatness," but it is still worship. It is the recognition by the observer of the value and greatness of the deeds done by the one who does them.

Here is the point: Man has been created with the capacity for worship. All men have it, saved or lost. Man was designed to see the greatness of his Creator and worship Him. Paul confirms this in Romans 1:20:

> "For since the creation of the world His invisible attributes, His eternal power and divine nature, have been clearly seen, being understood through what has been made...."

Paul also says this revelation leaves all men without excuse. What he means is that when we look at the creation around us, in all its glory and complexity, if we do not see the greatness of God, the problem is on our end, not God's. Paul also confirms that since the beginning, man has abused this capacity and used it to worship every kind of god imaginable, himself included.

> "For they (mankind) exchanged the truth of God for a

lie, and **worshiped and served the creature rather than the Creator,** who is blessed forever." —Romans 1:25

Clearly, something has gone terribly wrong. Can it be fixed? How? What did Lombardi do?

After one game in which the coach felt the Packers played particularly poorly, he came into the locker room after the game, called them all to attention, held up a football and said,

"Gentlemen, this is a football."

Sometimes, the only thing to do is start over. Go back to the basics. This is what winners do! In the Bible the "basics" begin with God: "In the beginning, God...." (Genesis 1:1). If you do not get it right at this point, nothing else matters.

So Who is God?

The Psalmist asks this supreme question. As Christians, we often think the most important question in life is, "Who is Jesus Christ?" But the truth is, Jesus is only important if we understand accurately who God is. Today, this is not a settled point. Many are now in the place where, at best, they are no longer sure; at worst, they no longer believe God matters. This is the one question that each of us must answer for ourselves. And we will all be accountable for our answer. The Psalmist answers for the Christian:

> "For who is God, but the LORD? And who is a rock,
> except our God."   —Psalm 18:31

The author of Hebrews makes it clear how crucial the answer is when he says, "And without faith it is impossible to please Him, for he who comes to God <u>must</u> believe that He is and that He is a rewarder of those who seek Him" (Hebrews 11:6).

The foundation of worship is, first, knowing, then believing and acting on the truth about who God really is. That knowledge is based on the truth God has revealed about Himself in the Bible. It was the early church father St. Augustine who so concisely encapsulated the idea that the Christian believes in order to know, he does not know in order to believe. (If you still have questions about who God is and whether Jesus Christ is God, I encourage you to read the Gospel of John. It reveals the uniqueness and deity of Christ like no other book.)

So we are left with a challenging dilemma. To know God requires divine revelation. The Bible teaches us that we cannot please God without faith, yet we can only know Him through faith. God only reveals Himself to faith. But if we reject faith as a legitimate path to truth, we have no way to find God, and no reason to worship Him. It is a self-made prison.

If the truth of who God is does not stir our hearts to worship Him, *it is simply because we do not see His greatness. We do not see that He is worthy of our worship.* There may be other causes, but this is the core problem.

Both Paul and the writer of Hebrews make it clear that the problem is not on God's end. God wants men and women to be able to recognize His greatness, to appreciate His goodness and love, to be motivated to love and serve Him. It is their blessing that the Father seeks. This can only happen when we truly know who God is. This kind of faith is not a "leap" into the dark unknown. There is evidence all around us.

To ensure there would be no misunderstanding, when God sent His Son, He sent One who would reveal to us the exact representation of God Himself in human form. As Jesus Himself said, "He who has seen Me has seen the Father." Paul added that in the creation you have the revelation of His eternal power and divine nature. Once you know and understand the astounding truth about who God is, you realize that those who do not see God's glory all around them are, just as the Bible says, blinded by the god of this world. They have to be blind not to see it. They may reject it, but God says they are now without excuse. One view is right and the other is wrong; there is no room to compromise (John 14:9; 2 Corinthians 4:4; Romans 1:20). Either they are true or not. But the question you have to decide is this:

Is God Real or Not? Does He Really Exist?

Just fifty years ago, to ask this question would get you a lot of amazed stares, people wondering how you could even ask the question. Not so today. It is an interesting facet of the Old Testament book of Judges that over and over again you see that it only takes one generation for an entire nation to forget God, to begin acting like He never existed. That was the case with Israel then, and today it seems America is on that same path.

But it has always been that way. The reason is simple. We are all sinners. We are born into this world with a nature that desires to be "independent" and free of all restraints. We want to acknowledge only one authority in our life: namely, our own.

Our modern, post-Christian culture feeds this desire. But as we will see in the next section, this culture is no accident. It has been designed by God's archenemy. It is his one great desire to see men reject God, reject His truth, reject His loving-kindness, and reject His salvation. He knows he can accomplish all these goals if he can generate a culture which at least despises God or, even better, does not even believe He exists.

It does not take a rocket scientist to see how successful the devil has been in this last generation. Our government and educational systems have all but outlawed God in our society. Those who still believe the Bible is God's Word, that it is absolute truth, are despised and ridiculed, most noticeably in the halls of higher education. My mentor, Joseph Carroll, used to call this "being educated into ignorance." But this is not all bad. Why?

It makes the line of demarcation separating those who truly belong to God and those who do not more and more clear. It means there is a cost to be reckoned with before one claims to be a follower of Christ. This has been a common theme throughout the history of the Church but, somehow, has almost disappeared in the experience of the Church in America (especially in the southern U. S. where *everyone* claims to be a Christian).

Once again the true followers of Christ are about to enter the ranks of those despised by the world. It will lead to some measure of suffering and persecution. The Scriptures promise that. But the Lord says that if it does, "Rejoice,"—you are in good company "for your reward in heaven is great; for in the same way they persecuted the prophets who were before you" (Matthew 5:12).

In other words, it is worth whatever price you will have to pay. God's glory is worth any price.

But the real question remains, "How did we get here?"

*   *   *   *   *

Once upon a time, we could truly be described as a Christian nation. It took President Obama to state the obvious. "Whatever we once were, we are no longer just a Christian nation; we are also a Jewish nation, a Muslim nation, a Buddhist nation, a Hindu nation, and a nation of non-believers" (FactCheck.org). This was meant to be something to be proud of, to glory in. But the truth is, this is a terrible indictment of just how far we have declined. Can you imagine the leader of a Muslim nation proudly proclaiming, "We are no longer just a Muslim nation, we are a nation of Jews, Christians and other infidels"? It is not going to happen. Why? Because they understand it as nothing to be proud of!

Many other faiths all claim to worship the same God as we do, but to them He is not the God and Father of our Lord Jesus Christ. The glory of America was that while holding to Christian principles as a nation, we graciously allowed those of other faiths to worship their god as they chose, without fear of retribution.

But again, the real question is, how did we get here? Why do so many Americans claim to be Christians, yet we seem to have so little impact on our nation and culture? How is that possible?

I believe the answer is simply that, as Christians, we have forgotten God. We have abandoned Him as the true guide of our lives, and the result is that He ceases to be real to us! He may still exist in theory; we may not actually deny Him, but He really has very little impact in our everyday lives. This is by no means unique to our generation. The history of the nation of Israel has many examples and reveals how easily and consistently it happens!

"Beware" of God's Blessing!

I know that sounds like a very strange statement, but again and again, it was God's warning to Israel. We see it over and over in the book of Deuteronomy.

"Beware that you do not forget the LORD your God by not keeping His commandments and His ordinances and His statutes which I am commanding you today; otherwise, when you have eaten and are satisfied, and have built good houses and lived in them, and when your herds and your flocks multiply, and your silver and gold multiply, and all that you have multiplies, then your heart will become proud and you will forget the LORD your God...."   —Deuteronomy 8:11-14

It is simply the natural tendency of the sin-polluted heart to forget the One who is the source of all our many blessings. The Psalmist encourages us to:

"Bless the Lord, O my soul, and all that is within me; bless His holy Name; Bless the Lord, O my soul, and forget none of His benefits."   —Psalm 103:1-2

The verses which follow these in Psalm 103 are a virtual laundry list of God's blessings, and they are tremendous blessings!

Clearly, there is no other person than God who can bestow these blessings. Why would we forget Him? The sad truth is that while we definitely want the blessings, we really do not appreciate (or at least have a lasting appreciation for) the One who made them possible! Yet it is often the loss of the blessings that teach us the value of the source of those blessings.

*   *   *   *   *

The Packers found this out when Lombardi resigned as head coach. Under him as coach, they never had a losing season; after him, they did not have another title for twenty-five years. They needed "the coach." He was the source of all the blessings and success they enjoyed.

This is why worship is so critical. As you study the Bible, especially the Old Testament, you will find again and again that one of the great tendencies of men is to forget God. And it is a costly error!

Over and over, God warns Israel to guard themselves against this. When Israel was about to follow Joshua into the Promised Land, after forty years of wilderness discipline, the message God gave Moses in the book of Deuteronomy to prepare Israel was filled with renewed warnings against forgetting God. Listen to Moses; this message is as vital to us today as it was to Israel.

> "Only give heed to yourself and keep your soul diligently, so that you *do not forget* the things which your eyes have seen and they do not depart from your heart all the days of your life; but make them known to your sons and your grandsons ..."
>
> —Deuteronomy 4:9 (also see 6:10-15)

Why is this so important? Because the promised blessings were coupled with terrible curses and punishment for disobedience. To forget God once He has begun to bless you inevitably leads to sin and more rebellion. Paul describes it in Romans 1 when he says, "...even though they knew God, they did not honor Him as God or give thanks...." (Romans 1:21).

The reality is that those who forget God perish. The danger seems to be at its greatest after we begin to experience His blessings! He alone is the Creator and Sustainer of all life. He alone is the source of all our blessings. To follow the path that leads to forgetting God is a path that can only lead to devastation in our lives.

Job 8:11, 13 says it well: "Can the papyrus grow up without a marsh? Can the rushes grow without water? So are the paths of all who **forget** God...."

Worship is the antidote to forgetting God. In order to worship from the heart, we need to see the greatness of God, we need Him to reveal Himself to us. How does He do this? C.S. Lewis summed it up well:

> *"It is in the process of being worshipped that God communicates His presence to men."*
> —Reflections on the Psalms

We need a fresh sense that "God is here," that He is present. Faith will allow Him to become "a living bright reality" in our lives. This will keep us "in the game" and in a place where we can hear His "still, small voice" call our name for the next play.

It is also true that much of our Christian life will be spent on *defense*, fending off enemy attacks trying to get us off the track of fulfilling the will of God for our life. Now it is time to see what God has done to arm us to stand against those attacks as He leads us to victory.

Offensive Strategy Summary:
Worship, Prayer, and the Word of God

1. Worship is *not* a ritual. Worship is the recognition of and inspired response to greatness. It is our response to what we see and understand of the goodness and greatness of God.

2. The Word of God is given that we might know Him. We master the truths of God's Word, not just for informational value, but for its eternal value.

3. If we are not awed by the knowledge of who God is and His greatness, the problem lies with us. What do we do? Go "back to basics." Go back to the beginning and start where God does, "In the beginning, God...."

4. Without faith in God, it is impossible to please Him. God only responds to faith. The truth about God is the only sure foundation for faith and worship. Faith honors God, worship exalts God, and the Bible is the only revelation of who He is.

5. If we are not careful, the blessings of God may result in our *forgetting* who the source of all our prosperity is. Worship is the ultimate antidote to the danger of forgetting God. People who see true greatness do not forget the one who is great. Worship constantly reminds us of God's greatness.

6. God desires us to come into His presence and bring all our petitions and requests. Prayer "in the Spirit," guided by the Spirit, allows us to participate with God in fulfilling His eternal purpose on earth, to seek and save that which was lost, the souls of men. This is His passion.

Chapter Sixteen

Iron-Man Defense:
The Strategy to Stop the Enemy

"Be on the alert, stand firm in the faith, act like men, be strong."

—1 Corinthians 16:13

Some believe that the best defense is a good offense. Others will say, "Defense is what wins championships." History tends to support the latter. You may have a super high-powered offense which is able to score lots of points most days, but if your defense cannot stop the opponent from scoring, then you really do not have an advantage.

But if your defense can keep the opponent's offense bottled up and off the field, you have a huge advantage. We saw this in the 2014 Super Bowl where the Seattle defense just overwhelmed the MVP Peyton Manning-led Denver offense. It was a classic case of the #1 Offense (Denver @ 35 pts/gm) against the #1 Defense (Seattle @ 14 pts/gm). Final score: 43-8. It was never really a contest.

Football illustrates a very important lesson for us. If the defense is able to stand firm against the offensive attempts of the enemy to distract, deceive, and distort, then victory is not only possible, it is likely. Not only will you keep the enemy from scoring, you will give your offense more opportunities to score. The key to a winning defense is to stand firm, don't give up the ground you have! This is as true in the spiritual realm as much as it is on NFL football fields. Defense is the key to winning and preparation is the key to its success.

Bart Starr said that the key to the Packers' success, the heart of Lombardi's game plan every week, was preparation. The ability to stand firm requires preparation. This is as true of defense as it is of offense; at least that was how Lombardi saw it. The apostle Paul evidently saw it the same way.

He wrote to Timothy to be ready in season and out of season, and to Titus to be ready for every good deed (2 Timothy 4:2; Titus 3:1). In other words, you are always to be ready so that when the attacks come (and they will!), you can defend your ground, and when opportunity presents itself, you can go on offense.

You cannot control when these opportunities come. Often we see them come in the form of what we call "divine appointments." But until then, we need to be prepared, standing firm.

It should be obvious, but we must constantly remind ourselves that this is Iron-Man Christianity. You are *always* on offense or defense, you are never a spectator or out of the game! But how do we get prepared?

"Stand Firm"...with the Team

In the last chapter of his epistle to the Ephesians, the apostle Paul gives us a strong visual illustration of what a solid winning defense looks like in the Christian's life. Since Paul was literally in chains in a prison house at Rome, surrounded by Roman soldiers at the time he wrote this letter, it is quite natural that he would use the Roman soldier's armor as a picture of the Christian soldier's armor. Everyone who read it 2000 years ago would immediately grasp the illustration and understand it. Roman soldiers were not only tough, they were always ready to fight!

Paul's letter to the Ephesians is filled with an unusual amount of lofty spiritual truths we find nowhere else in the Bible. He begins before the foundation of the world, with what God has sovereignly done in and through Christ. He reveals how it was all planned in eternity. He then goes on to show our helpless need of a Savior and how God accomplished that saving work, both individually and corporately, in the uniting of both Jews and Gentiles into a "new creation" we call the body of Christ, the Church.

In chapters 4 and 5, Paul gives the practical application of these truths. He tells us what our lives are to look like because of what God has done for us in Christ. The obvious lesson is that we have a new power working in us and we are to use it, not for our own selfish ambitions, but to work to see these same life-transforming truths brought to fruit in ourselves and in those around us, especially our family in Christ. This lesson permeates the New Testament. It is as a team working together in unity that we can make the greatest impact on the enemy in this world. Alone we can do very little.

The Reality of Spiritual Warfare

In the last half of Ephesians 6, Paul details a reality that most of us are only vaguely conscious of in our day, namely, God has an enemy. He has opposed God since before this world began. He hates God and he hates anyone who is identified with God. Since we are followers of Christ that means us. He cannot really fight against God directly, so he sets his sights on us, doing all he can to destroy or at least minimize our impact on this world, his world.

Remember, he (Satan) is the "god" of this world. Adam yielded his authority to the devil when he rebelled against God in the Garden of Eden. While the devil only has limited power, his power and authority on this earth are very real, at least for now. The war between God and the devil, between the forces of good and evil, are ongoing. It is, in the truest sense, a "death match," even if most people are totally ignorant of them.

Paul sees this opposition as warfare. It comes most powerfully in the form of what we call temptations to sin. We all experience temptation. Even Christ Himself was sorely tempted. Temptation usually comes in one of three basic forms: the lust of the flesh, the lust of the eyes, and the pride of life (1 John 2:16). You may be tempted by all of these or just one or two. That depends on your temperament and personality. Some people are weak in some areas but not others. Make no mistake though, the devil has a good idea where you will be weakest and he is a master at figuring out the most opportune time to attack. So how do we defend ourselves?

The Iron-Man Christian's Defense: Some "Basics"

In Ephesians 6, he uses the Roman soldier's armor as his example. He exhorts us "...put on the full armor of God...." —to what purpose? "...that you may be able to stand firm against the schemes of the devil." Notice three things here:

1. It is the armor of God.

God knows His enemy is going to attack us. But He has not left us defenseless. Paul exhorts us in verse 10 to be strong in the Lord and in the strength of His might.

Our success is rooted in the strength of the one we are now united to, namely, the Lord Himself!

To fight the devil in our own strength is useless and futile, even foolish. God's armor has every element we need to defeat the enemy. This is full spiritual armor!

2. Success is defined as "standing firm."

This is very important! Your goal in defense is simply to stand firm. If you do that, you have won the battle! Please read that again. When the enemy attacks you, it is not time for offense. It is time to stand firm, resist him. James 4 tells us to resist the devil, and he will flee from us. This is the goal. Do not complicate it. Use the weapons God has given us and having done all, stand firm.

Note the words, "having done all" in v. 13. What does this mean? Some Bibles translate it "having done everything." The idea here is preparation. What that meant was studying the enemy. In order to study the enemy wisely, you have to know why he does what he does.

3. The attacks will come in the form of "schemes" (v.11).

Schemes is another word for strategies. What are strategies based on? Think about this.

Key: Your Game Plan/Strategy is based on what you believe are weaknesses in your opponent's defense.

Guess what? Your opponent's strategies are based on the same thing—what he believes are your weaknesses in your defense! Lombardi was not a whiz with defensive strategies. What he learned came mostly from Tom Landry when they both coached with the New York Giants.

Landry was the innovator on defensive strategies. Lombardi hired the best defensive coaches he could in Phil Bengston and Norb Hecker (both went on to be NFL head coaches). He taught them all what he had gleaned from Tom Landry in New York, then drove them mercilessly to study and prepare their defenses for each game the way he did for the offense. The goal, as always, was to stand firm. Their record proves they were pretty successful.

Preparing Your Defense

In the Christian's life, **preparation** is going to require diligence and honesty.

First, you have to grasp and understand that while your enemy is not God, he is a real and powerful enemy. You can stand firm against him, thwart his attempts to overwhelm you, but only

God's power can defeat him. In the final battle, the Lord Jesus will do just this. In the interim, as the apostle Peter puts it, "...[Y]our adversary, the devil, prowls around like a roaring lion, seeking someone (i.e., you!) to devour. But <u>resist</u> him, <u>firm</u> in your faith...." (1 Peter 5:8-9a).

If a lion were in your backyard, you would not treat him like a pet, would you? The devil is like having a lion in your backyard. Treat him with caution and resist the temptations he throws at you. You cannot defeat him on your own.

Paul says, "...be strong in the Lord...in the strength of His might" (Ephesians 6:10).

Second, know that the enemy is going to tempt you based on *what he perceives are your weaknesses.* What do you think he sees? You better assume that just like the Packers had game film on all their opponents, the devil has "game film" on your life. He has studied you and knows what you do and when you do it. What does he know? What has he seen?

He is not omniscient, but if your heart is set to seek the Lord, if you are determined to follow Him and do His will, then you are a threat to him. You can bet he has enough "game film" on you to figure out where <u>you</u> are likely to be most vulnerable.

This means you have to be honest with yourself and with God. It has been well said, "We need to keep short accounts with God." This also means we have to honestly look at our lives and call sin what it is. God already knows what it is; He is not deceived, even if you are. He will also not be mocked.

But He will be gracious to forgive us, if we own up to it and confess it with a repentant heart. If we do not, we will be guilty of harboring that sin—and end up giving the devil an obvious attack point. Lust, lies, guilt, an unforgiving spirit, relationships or friendships you know are not ones that encourage you to honor God—you know whatever it is in your life. The devil knows this as well. He just does not want you to believe he knows it. You need to deal with it before the devil uses it to derail you. Confess it, accept God's total forgiveness, turn from it and put on the armor God has provided for your defense.

You have to stay in the game to win!

So let's look at the armor God has given us.

Chapter Seventeen

The Iron-Man's Complete Armor

"For in Him all the fullness of Deity dwells...
and in Him <u>you</u> have been made complete..."
—Colossians 2:9-10a

Every Saturday and Sunday, football players in both college and the NFL put on armor just like ancient Roman soldiers did before they headed to the field to do battle. They put on spiked shoes, shoulder pads, hip pads, and helmets. Some even put on flak jackets for protection! The goal of all this gear, all this protective equipment, is to keep them from getting knocked out of the game through injuries. God does not want the Christian disciple to get knocked out of the game either. The apostle Paul describes the preparation necessary for the Christian to do battle. He uses the Roman soldier's armor as his model.

In Ephesians 6, Paul describes in vivid detail the seven pieces that make up the complete armor God has provided for the Christian's defense. He begins right in the middle, where our physical strength lies. Let's go through the picture and try to capture Paul's vision of the Christian soldier.

He begins in verse 14 by saying, "Stand firm therefore, having..." I want you to note that the first three things Paul tells us to appropriate for our defense, he uses the word "having." "*Having* girded your loins with truth...*having* put on the breastplate of righteousness...*having* shod your feet...."

The point is this: before you can stand firm in your defense against the enemy, you must have already done certain things; after the game is over it is too late.

I did something similar when I played football. As a wide receiver, I would put on a "flak jacket" to protect my core muscles and organs. I needed to put it on before the game; after the game it would do me no good. It was part of my game preparation.

What things does the Christian need to do to be prepared on defense?

First, Paul begins with **"having girded your loins with truth..."**

What does this mean? The loins include the thighs and the lower abdomen. These are the strongest muscles in the body. Anyone who has ever pulled or torn a hamstring muscle knows that if this happens, your movement is severely limited, and a move with power is almost impossible.

There is also a second picture here which is important. In biblical/Roman Empire days, the typical clothing for men included a tunic and a long flowing robe. If you were attacked and had to move quickly, you would gather the folds of the robe and loop them through the belt which girded your loins. This allowed swift, unimpeded movement. Truth is not only the key to protecting your strength, it also allows swift, unimpeded movement when you are under attack.

The truth we are describing here is not what is often called conventional wisdom. That is what the world calls truth. It is the current collection of wisdom derived from the faulty thinking of sin-polluted minds. It changes often as apparently new and better wisdom emerges. In reality, it is totally unreliable. The truth of which Paul speaks here is objective truth, it is truth revealed by God and recorded in the Bible.

It is truth which sanctifies, sets followers of Christ apart from everyone else. It is truth which never, ever changes, regardless of the situation or circumstances.

Man did not think up the truths in the Bible. You can see this contrast quite clearly if you just stop and compare the attributes of the so-called Greek gods with the attributes which God has revealed about Himself in Scripture. The difference is stark.

The Greek god often had a gift or special power, but also many of the flaws and failings of human beings. The true God is the epitome of grace, kindness, love, and humility. A Greek god has actually never been seen on earth; they were a myth, a figment of the imagination. The other (Jesus Christ) has been revealed from heaven and His glory was seen on earth. By His perfect life, He overcame death and offers eternal life to those who will follow Him. One is really nothing more than a fictional superman, at best. The other is the "one, true and living God." If you do not have this understanding and belief as the anchor and foundation of your faith in God, you will not be able to stand against the devil.

We need to be constantly aware that we live in a day when absolutes and those who believe in them are despised. To believe that God actually created this world opens you to ridicule as ignorant or worse. Mark it down, as we said earlier, the destiny of your life will be determined by your view of the first verse in

Genesis. Either it is true and God supernaturally created the world out of nothing, or evolution, a big "bang," or some other chance event is responsible for our existence. One thing is sure, one group of "believers" is made up of fools and the other group of wise men. There is no other option. Which group are you in? Your choice will determine the path of your life.

Second, Paul says we need to **"put on the breastplate of Righteousness."**

What is he saying? The warring soldier's breastplate covered all his vital organs (heart, lungs, liver, etc.). If any one of these organs is pierced through, death is virtually inevitable. Conversely, you can experience injury to almost every other part of the body and survive. The meaning here is pretty simple.

The "breastplate of righteousness" is the righteousness of Christ; it is **not** our righteousness! Righteousness before God can only come from living a perfect life. It is not a *best effort*; trying to "do good" does not cut it. Why? Because the standard is perfection! For us, it is an impossible standard. That is why Jesus came. Jesus Christ lived a perfect life, died on the Cross, and rose again. It was not possible for death to hold Him in the grave. Why? Paul says in 2 Corinthians 5:21, "...He made Him who knew no sin to be sin on our behalf..." Why? So that we might become the righteousness of God in Him.

Here is the point: we have no righteousness of our own. Our sinful lives have ruined that possibility. But in order to have an eternal relationship with God, we have to be as righteous as He is. You would say that is impossible. And you are right! Based on our own righteous deeds we would be doomed. But God has made it possible that the penalty for our sins could be paid by another:

His Son. The Lord Jesus Christ lived a perfectly sinless life, then offered that life as payment for the sins of the whole world. God declared the sufficiency and divine acceptance of that sacrifice when He raised Him from the dead. Hallelujah! Sin is finished.

Now when we put our faith and trust completely in what He did, God credits the righteousness of Jesus' life to us. We trust in His righteousness, not our own. Our faith allows a union to be formed between Jesus Christ and us that is eternally secure. God sees us as He sees His Son. God's sanctifying purpose on this earth is to make us like His Son so that we may enjoy this relationship to the fullest throughout eternity.

We must be armed with the knowledge of the sufficiency of our Savior's sacrifice for our sins and our complete trust in it for our salvation. To doubt this truth or not to know it will leave us vulnerable to attack. With it, we are fully protected against the enemy's accusations of our guilt and rightful condemnation.

Everything the devil accuses us of will be true. We know we have done these sinful deeds; our conscience will testify to it. We are guilty. What our accuser will not say is, "Jesus paid it all for you." With the penalty paid, God is free to pardon us. And He has. That is our defense.

Long ago, the Moravian Count Nicholas Zinzendorf summed it all up beautifully in this hymn:

> Jesus Thy blood and righteousness,
> My beauty are, my glorious dress;
> Midst flaming worlds, in these arrayed,
> With joy shall I lift up my head.

Lord I believe were sinners more
Than sand upon the ocean's shore,
Thou hast for all a ransom paid,
For all a full atonement made.

Third, Paul says we must have our feet "**shod with the preparation of the gospel of peace.**"

The enemy would like to have us believe that our war is with God; that He is angry and wants vengeance against sinners for their rebellion. The truth is that our sin has caused a separation between God and us, but that is only a partial truth. The whole truth is that Christ has reconciled to God all those who put their faith in Him. As Paul joyously concludes in Romans 5:1-2,

> "Therefore, having been justified by faith, we have peace
> with God through our Lord Jesus Christ, through whom
> also we have obtained our introduction by faith into this
> grace in which we stand; and we exult in hope of the glory
> of God."

The war is over! Peace reigns in righteousness and our lives are eternally blessed in Christ. This is the message we have to share with the whole world. Only those who reject His offer of reconciliation will fall into the "hands of an angry God." Do you see the difference? Are you prepared to share it?

Fourth, Paul says, "**take up the shield of faith with which you will be able to extinguish all the flaming missiles (KJV: fiery darts) of the evil one.**"

Every soldier in Rome had two weapons: a sword and a shield. In ancient and medieval warfare, when you wanted to attack an enemy you would often make your first attack using arrows. Today, we use the same strategy; we just drop bombs instead of arrows. Most people have seen the movie *Braveheart*. When the Scots lined up against the British, the first line of attack was a salvo of arrows, often flaming missiles to be lobbed down on the enemy. The Scottish answer was simply to lift up the shields and cover themselves with it until the attack was over. Why do they do this? Because it works! Please also note this: It would have done them no good to have the shield but not lift it to cover themselves when they were attacked.

The enemy may launch direct attacks at us individually or at the Church as a whole (as in times when it is under persecution), but if the arrow is stopped with the shield, it cannot harm us.

The Christian's shield is his faith, His trust in God. The devil knows he cannot defeat God, so he attacks our faith. Why?

The Goal is always Doubt.

The devil knows that if he can cause us to doubt the truth of God's Word, then we become vulnerable to his temptations. Faith and doubt cannot coexist. Once we doubt God or, as the apostle James says, become "double-minded," we are facing the enemy in our own strength (or more accurately, our really pathetic weakness). This is exactly what he did to Adam and Eve in the Garden of Eden.

The Source of Sin

When you read the first two chapters of Genesis, you cannot help but see that God was designing an incredibly delightful place for Adam to live, a place where God and Adam could enjoy life together. The plan was to enjoy it forever. Remember, before sin came into the world, there was no death. Adam would never have died if he had not believed the devil's lies about God.

Death is the result of sin. Sin is the result of believing a lie about God. How can you believe in someone for salvation whom you do not trust?

Why does the devil so often attack at this point? For the same reason the Packers continually ran the "power sweep," it worked! You run a play until it does not work anymore. That is just common sense. Those who think the devil is a fool often pay for it dearly.

What does the devil most want us to doubt about God? Some may argue here, but I believe the one thing the devil most wants us to doubt is God's goodness. This has to be the cornerstone of your relationship with God. Either you believe that He is essentially good or He is not. When we say "essentially good," we mean that in His own being there is no evil, none at all (as the Bible says, in Him there is no darkness at all), and that all His motivations are pure and designed for our benefit and well-being and, ultimately, our joy.

To put it in simpler and very much New Testament terms, God loves and cares for us as a perfect loving Father would for his own son. Sometimes this means disciplining us, which usually is not pleasant. In those moments, the devil would tell us that a loving God would not be so hard on us. That He really does not love us; He may not even like us! After all, look at your life, what is there to love? He has a point.

But the enemy's strategy will only work if we do not know God's answer to it, which is what? It is what Christ has done for us. If we raise that shield of faith, the devil loses.

At the right moment (and the devil is a master at knowing

when to attack us!), these fiery darts can come at us like "flaming missiles" with one goal: to attack and destroy our faith in God. When that happens, we need to be ready to raise the shield of faith in defense. We need to know in our hearts that while we did fall terribly short, Jesus loved us anyway and died for us, so our past sinful life is gone. God has promised it will never be brought up again by Him. This is the truth of God's Word. If we believe what He has said, we will not be vulnerable to this attack.

*   *   *   *   *

Sometimes, these attacks will come in the form of "bad things happening to good people"—such as when a young child seems to randomly die of a terrible, painful disease; or when a lunatic goes on a shooting spree, and a young mother and child are senselessly killed. Or when a terrorist unleashes a toxic, lethal gas and multitudes of innocent people die. The point is, events like these prove evil is alive and well. So the argument goes: IF God is really good, why does He allow this evil to exist. And of course, why does He allow it to damage or destroy "good" people's lives especially if the evil touches us?

These kinds of attacks can be very effective in challenging our faith, especially when we are the mother of the child dying of cancer or the husband of the wife and child who are shot. We have to make it our number one priority to know God and His "essential" goodness; to deeply and intimately know His ways and character, so that we can raise the shield of faith in confidence, even when we do not understand the seemingly senseless situation He has allowed into our lives. When life seems unfair, the shield of faith in God must be raised to defend us.

At times like these, the lesson of Job can be a real anchor. He was faithful and upright; God Himself acknowledged this. Yet God let his life be virtually destroyed. Why? There was a greater purpose, the glory of God, and Job was the battlefield, though he never knew it. The Bible says, "Through all this Job did not sin or blame God." How did he win? He stood firm.

Remember: the victory is won by simply "standing firm" in the face of the onslaught. If we don't yield to the devil's doubts, we win.

Fifth, Paul exhorts us to **"take the helmet of salvation."**

The head controls everything. It has the mind, the eyes, the ears, and the voice. A blow to the head can knock you unconscious, totally neutralizing your effectiveness on the battlefield, or you can easily be killed. The helmet helps protect from those blows.

The meaning of the "helmet of salvation" goes farther than this picture will allow. The Roman soldier's helmet cannot ultimately protect you from physical death in this life any more than it could the Roman soldier. What the biblical helmet does offer is absolute protection for your soul and spirit.

The eternal parts of your life can never be destroyed by evil once you put on the helmet of salvation. The reason is simple. You are sealed by the Holy Spirit; you have died and your life is hidden with Christ in God (Ephesians 1:13; Colossians 3:3). And Jesus said, "He (the devil) has nothing in Me..." (John 14:30). Always remember, you are eternally secure in Christ. Why?

Regardless of what happens to your physical body on this earth (which is going to die one day, one way or another anyway!) nothing can touch what belongs to God in Christ! Paul says, "You are not your own, you have been bought with a price...." What does that mean?

It means that God owns us now. If we belong to Christ, He has the title deed to our lives. Once the battle was *for* your soul, now it is *against* your soul. Before, you did not even know there was a battle going on, now you have the privilege and obligation to win other souls for Christ.

So far, we have five pieces of the armor: Truth, Righteousness, the Gospel, the Shield of Faith and the Helmet of Salvation. What is missing? Weapons. And God has given the most powerful weapon of all: Himself!

Chapter Eighteen

The Iron-Man Weapons of the Spirit

"Satan trembles when he sees the weakest saint upon his knees."
—William Cowper

T he last two pieces of the Christian's defense arsenal are actually weapons used on both offense and defense; the "Sword of the Spirit, which is the Word of God" and "Prayer...in the Spirit."

The "Sword of the Spirit"

In the section on "Iron-Man Offense," we have dealt with the importance and necessity of the Christian soldier knowing and trusting the Word of God as revealed in the Scriptures. It is God's Word to us. It is alive and powerful (Hebrews 4:12). It contains what He has to say about our lives, how we are to live those lives, and what their primary purpose is. In that context, think about these words of Christ Himself and their meaning. "He (Jesus) said, 'Who are My mother and My brothers?' Looking about at those who were sitting around Him, He said,

'Behold My mother and My brothers! For whoever does the will of God, he is My brother and sister and mother'" (Mark 3:34-35).

Mark it down! This is going to be one of the enemy's primary targets and the place where you will have to make your stand. The enemy will do everything he can to keep you from doing the will of God! Why? This defeats God's entire purpose for your life.

We live in a day when many in the Church simply want everyone to "believe...believe...believe." The enemy has made great use of this teaching. Why? Because, while it is true, it is only a half-truth. The way it is most often presented puts the emphasis on the intellectual acceptance of biblical facts as the basis of salvation. There is no call to commitment, no call to dedication, no call to "Follow Me."

While it is absolutely true that you are not saved by commitment or dedication (you are saved by grace through faith (Ephesians 2:8), what other manifestation of true faith (i.e., trust) is there? The saving faith which is the gift of God will always manifest itself in action. What action? The desire to know and do the will of God. In our zeal to keep the gospel free of "works," we have gone to the other extreme.

The Bible also clearly teaches in James 2:14, 26 that faith without works is dead, period.

*　　*　　*　　*　　*

This is a grave error. If our faith is really only an intellectual act, it does not produce biblical salvation. Biblically, salvation is **not** simply justification by faith; it is justification, sanctification and ultimate glorification with Christ. You either get all of it or none of it. In the Bible, saving faith always produces a "new birth," what Paul calls a "new creation." This is what Jesus told

Nicodemus, "You must be born again." True repentance and faith produce not just a changed life, but a new life, a life that could never have been lived before God came to dwell in that person (Romans 6:4).

If faith is not followed by action, it is not alive, it is not living faith. But what kind of action?

The simplest, clearest manifestation of a person being born again is the desire and determination to know and do the will of God. Before conversion, the mindset of the unregenerate man is very obvious. His attitude toward God is my will (not "Thy will") be done. He is selfish and primarily consumed with satisfying the lusts of his flesh, whatever they may be. He knows nothing else.

According to the apostle Paul in Romans 8, the mindset of the lost man is hostile toward God; he refuses to accept the law of God, he is not even able to do so. It is literally against his nature; he is a rebel. But the new man in Christ has a new purpose in life. Both the apostles Peter and John say the same thing.

> "Therefore, since Christ has suffered in the flesh, arm yourselves also with the same purpose, because he who has suffered in the flesh has ceased from sin, so as to live the rest of the time in the flesh no longer for the lusts of men, but for the will of God. For the time past is sufficient for you to have carried out the desire of the Gentiles, having pursued a course of sensuality, lusts, drunkenness, carousing, drinking parties and abominable idolatries."　　　　　—1 Peter 4:1-3

> "Do not love the world nor the things in the world. If anyone loves the world, the love of the Father is not in him. For all that is in the world, the lust of the flesh and the lust of the eyes and the boastful pride of life, is

not from the Father, but is from the world. The world
is passing away, and also its lusts; but the one who does
the will of God lives forever."   —1 John 2:15-17

The new life has a new purpose, a new goal. Why is this so important?

You cannot stand against an enemy if you do not know which side you are on, and why you are fighting! God does not leave us ignorant. We are not slaves, we are now brothers-in-arms with Christ. Once we were enemies of God, now we are bond-servants. He has enlisted us to carry on the battle and finish what He began.

What is the will of God? What is the will of God for your life? Do you see these as two separate questions? Your answer will reveal how much you understand about the will of God—and what is most important to Him. It will also reveal the ultimate priority in your life. These are critical questions, yet very few young people are being challenged with them.

Knowing the Will of God

To ever understand what the will of God is for your life (the *micro* view), you must first understand the ultimate purpose and will of God (the *macro* view). Why? Because your individual life mission has to be guided by the ultimate mission purpose of God, just as the individual player's assignment has to fit in with the ultimate game plan of his head coach. It does no good for a pulling guard to decide on his own to block a different man than he was assigned to block; his missed block will likely result in a loss on the play...and a very unhappy coach! But what is God's plan?

Jesus said, "For the Son of Man has come to seek and to save that which was lost" (Luke 19:10). Again in Luke 4:18, "The Spirit of the LORD is upon Me, because He anointed Me to preach the gospel to the poor. He has sent Me to proclaim release to the captives."

Jesus was clear about His mission from God, "I must preach the kingdom of God to the other cities also for I was sent for this purpose" (Luke 4:43).

He was also clear that fulfilling His mission for His Father meant His death on the cross.

> "Now My soul has become troubled; and what shall I say, 'Father, save Me from this hour?' But for this purpose I came to this hour. Father, glorify Your name." —John 12:27-28

So God's Plan for us is the same plan He had for His Son: "...as the Father has sent Me, I also send you" (John 20:21b).

His Mission is Now Our Mission

We cannot miss this point and ever find or fulfill God's purpose for our lives. God's Plan is His Son. God's Plan for us is to listen to Him and to follow Him. God has made Him both Lord and Christ. He is the head of the Church; He is the head coach! The Scriptures are clear on this.

> "For you have been called for this purpose, since Christ also suffered for you, leaving you an example for you to follow in His steps." —1 Peter 2:21

> "This is My beloved Son, with whom I am well-pleased; listen to Him!" —Matthew 17:5

After the Resurrection, things really got interesting! No one had ever risen from the dead (excluding the miracles of Jesus), but many people did believe in ghosts, especially evil spirits. As we might say in our modern vernacular, this was a day when Jesus rocked their world. And they really did not know how to react. How would you have reacted?

> "Jesus came and stood in their midst and said to them, 'Peace be with you.' And when He had said this, He showed them both His hands and His side. The disciples then rejoiced when they saw the Lord. So Jesus said to them again, 'Peace be with you; **as the Father has sent Me, I also send you**." —John 20:19, 21

Two things to note here, Jesus understood their concerns, He did not ignore them. He reassured them by showing it was really Him, alive from the dead, the wounds still visible. Twice He said, "Peace be with you." Now they could rejoice. Why? If He could overcome death, was there anything He could not accomplish? The answer is obviously, "No."

The other point relates to our question concerning the will of God for us. Here Jesus answers it. With all the authority of One who has overcome the greatest enemy of all He says, "As the Father has sent Me, I also send you." In His first official act as the risen, conquering King, Jesus issues the divine decree authorizing His disciples to go into the world and finish what He began, "seeking and saving that which was lost." How would they do that? By making disciples. It has always been true— discipleship is the most biblical form of evangelism.

"And Jesus came up and spoke to them, saying, 'All authority has been given to Me in heaven and on earth. Go therefore and **make disciples of all the nations, baptizing them...teaching them to observe all that I commanded you**; and lo, I am with you always, even to the end of the age.'" —Matthew 28:18-20

That is the plan. Any consideration of your plan for your life has to fit into the context of the ultimate divine plan: making disciples of Jesus Christ, anywhere and everywhere, teaching them what He has taught us. Where and in what position does God want you to play in that? If you ever want to truly find satisfaction in your life, you must find out that answer for yourself.

How? By being prepared and then available to the Coach when he calls. Are you ready? Is your heart set to do the will of God? If so, make no mistake, **He will be calling you!**

Wherever it is and whatever it is, you are going to need God's power to do God's work. It cannot be done by human strength! That is why He told the disciples to wait for that power after He rose from the dead, "...for you shall receive power when the Holy Spirit has come upon you...." (Acts 1:8).

"Prayer in the Spirit"

The Holy Spirit is the power of God in man. When the Bible says Christ "is in you," it means that the Spirit of Christ has literally come to indwell the one who has repented and put his total trust in Christ. In doing so He makes us one in spirit with Christ. By His enabling power, we can now fulfill the purpose of God by doing the will of God in the power of God.

Whether it is praying in the Spirit, walking in the Spirit, or living by the Spirit, it is all about the new life in the Holy Spirit which has caused us to be born again, to become "new creations" as Paul describes us to the Corinthians. It is our spiritual union with God which is now the most powerful weapon in our arsenal. It is by God working through us that His power is seen most readily on the earth. We are His hands and feet, and we are the "salt and light" of the Sermon on the Mount. It is an awesome responsibility; and with great privilege comes great responsibility.

This we should already know, but it bears repeating. The Holy Spirit is the third person of the Trinity. He is omniscient, omnipotent, and omnipresent. He is God's power in us and through us to the world.

He is the reason that the Word of God is not just words on paper. He is the reason that the Word of God is alive and powerful. He is the reason that the gospel is the power of God unto salvation. It is His divinely appointed task to be the power enabling us to finish the ministry of Christ on this earth. We are the ones who are to preach the truth of the gospel, but He alone is the One who can open blind eyes and soften hardened hearts so the "precious seed" can be sown and souls harvested. We plow and sow, but He alone can give life.

Paul exhorts us to take up...the Sword of the Spirit which is the Word of God and to pray in the Spirit. Why? How do we use this when we are on defense? Why is this the ultimate weapon against the devil? Because it brings the power of God and the truth of God into the battle. Truth is the ultimate weapon against liars, and much of our spiritual battle will involve resisting the lies of the devil.

"Lies, Lies, Lies"

In John 8, Jesus has a particularly intense exchange with Jews who were unable to grasp the truth of what He was saying to them. They were trying to accuse Him of some sin which would justify their killing Him. He knew this. But more than this, He knew who was behind it—the devil. He said,

> "You are of your father the devil, and you want to do the desires of your father. He was a murderer from the beginning, and does not stand in the truth because there is no truth in him. Whenever he speaks a lie, he speaks from his own nature, for he is a liar and the father of lies."   —John 8:44

A lie may be an outright denial of the truth or it may be a distortion of the truth or it may be a subtle twisting of the truth intended to deceive us. In the passage in John 8 cited above, the Lord says that IF you know the truth, really know and embrace the truth, "the truth shall set you free." Why is that true? Is it really true?

One reason it is true is simply because the person who knows the truth is not vulnerable to lies. If he is not sure of the truth, he can still be deceived, but when faced directly with the truth and a lie about the truth, he knows the difference. If you do not know what the truth is, you are totally defenseless. And the devil will be merciless in his attacks.

What lies will the devil use? The same ones he used when he tempted the Lord in the wilderness. How did the Lord defeat him? Using the same weapons He has given us. Let's see the real head coach in action.

Chapter Nineteen

The First Iron-Man Battle:
The Lord is Challenged

"Some men want to live within the sound of a church or chapel bell; I want to run a rescue mission within a yard of hell."

—C. T. Studd

In chapter four of both the gospels of Luke and Matthew, the devil's temptation of the Lord in the wilderness is recorded. Three temptations are mentioned. From these records, we can and should note several things.

1. **The devil is real**. The devil is not just a personification of an evil "force." He is the living, active, and personal ruler of this world. He is also the enemy of God. At this moment (within the boundaries which God has allowed), the devil has authority over this world. He has personally come to try to tempt Jesus into sin.

2. **Jesus was in the will of God**. The Scripture is unequivocal. Jesus was led by the Spirit into the wilderness for the purpose of His being tempted (Matthew 4:1). Is it possible that God purposely allows us to be tempted? Does He want us to sin? These are two different questions. The answer to the first is yes.

The answer to the second is no. This test was to prove that Jesus was a worthy man, that He would not collapse under the pressure of Satan's temptations and that His sacrifice of Himself would be that of one whose life was "unblemished, spotless," sinless and perfect. He was the perfect sacrifice for sin; He was tested and proven worthy.

3. **Temptation is *not* sin.** We need to make sure we understand this. To be tempted is not a sin. It is our response to the tempting that can become sin, or it can prove that we chose to honor God and not sin. Without the test, we do not know for sure. For the follower of Christ, temptations are meant to be tests of faith. All of us will be tested. Sometimes the tests will be very, very difficult. The follower of Christ has to view these as tests of faith, and by overcoming them, their faith is strengthened.

The apostle James says, "...the testing of your faith produces **endurance**. And let endurance have its perfect result, that you may be perfect and complete, lacking in nothing" (James.1:3-4). The man or woman whose faith in God is strong is not only precious to God, they will be very useful to God in fulfilling the mission of Christ.

Think of it this way. Who is more valuable to the Army general: the new recruit who is untried and untested, or the battlefield-tested veteran who has experienced victory? It is the same way on the football field. In whom is the coach going to be more confident: the rookie QB who is still stunned by how fast things happen at the professional level or the seasoned veteran who has led the team to many victories? It is not really different in the gospel mission. God uses the one who He knows will do His will and trust Him in doing it. When adversity comes, he will not waver in unbelief. Why? He knows God is faithful to His Word.

The Forms of Temptations

If Jesus is our pattern for facing and overcoming the devil, we should note this: Jesus did not try to outsmart the devil. He simply responded with truth, the Word of God. He did not try to create a new play. By now we should know what Vince Lombardi would have said to his players if, rather than running the play he called, they just decided to run something they came up with. They would be sitting on the bench—and getting an earful!

God has given us a playbook. Jesus was intimately familiar with it; He had been since He was a young boy. He did not try to change it, He skillfully wielded the weapon He knew best and knew worked.

Jesus lived by two principles: *God is faithful* and *the Word of God is truth*. These principles sustained Him and they will sustain us, if we determine to live by them. If we set ourselves to do the will of God, victory is assured. That is not a misprint. Victory is certain!

The question then is, in what form will the devil's temptations come to us?

There are a lot of variations! The interesting thing is they all seem to begin with the letter D. These are some of the major categories:

Doubt–Deception–Delusion–Disappointment–Discouragement

Your particular circumstances, personality, and temperament will often determine which flavor of temptation the devil decides to use to tempt you. **But the underlying goal of virtually every temptation is to get you to doubt God—especially His goodness**, in some way or other.

This is where he began with Adam and Eve in the garden. Ultimately he wanted them to doubt God's goodness. He wanted them to believe God was withholding something; that something was missing which would make their lives much better. In fact, they would be like God! Eve, Paul says, was deceived by this deception.

The devil did not change the play when he tempted Jesus. All three temptations are built around one word, "IF." "If" immediately introduces the idea of doubt, that something may not be true.

Important Note: What did the Lord do to defeat the devil? Did He use His divine power? Did He call down a legion of angels? No. What He did was very simple. He stood firm on God's Word. Let's not miss this.

Key Point: Jesus defeated the devil by simply "standing firm" on God's Word.

Like the Packers, the devil has a "power sweep" play that works almost every time. His goal is simply to introduce doubt into our minds. Faith and doubt cannot coexist together. To Jesus, he said "If" three times. The temptations he used are very instructive for us. He will use them on us also.

*   *   *   *   *

Temptations are often described as and come in some form of "lust of the flesh, lust of the eyes and the pride of life." Their source will normally be found in the world, the flesh or the devil himself.

Temptation #1—The temptation to turn stones to bread. The lust of the flesh.

Jesus was hungry. Hunger is a perfectly legitimate need (especially after 40 days of fasting). The Father had always provided for His Son's needs, but now He was hungry and there was no provision, at least not yet. This was an opportunity in Satan's mind. An opportunity to introduce doubt. About what? About the Father's faithfulness and goodness.

But there was another, more subtle angle to this. When Satan said, "If you are the Son of God"—he was not trying to challenge Him to prove His deity. What he was really doing was tempting Jesus' ego. In effect, what he was saying was, "If You are the Son of God, You do not need to wait on God to provide; You can easily provide for Yourself. You can decide for yourself when it is time to eat and how to provide it. You decide."

At that point, Jesus had to decide whether to do what He wanted or do His Father's will. You cannot act independently of God and still claim to do His will. That is why Jesus said that His life depended on more than just physical food. His inner life, His spiritual life depended on His trusting His Father, living "on every word that proceeds out of the mouth of God." Jesus stood firm on the truth that God is faithful, and Satan was defeated. Then His physical need was met.

Temptation #2—The temptation to throw Himself down from the temple and trust God to save Him.

Again, the challenge is "If"—if you are the Son of God and if You are going to live on God's Word, then prove it. IF You are the Son of God, then throw yourself down. Why? Because the Scriptures say that God has ordained angelic protection that would keep Him from harm.

But that protection is ordained only as long as He is doing the will of His Father. Again, the temptation is to act independently, in this case to presumptuously force God's hand to do something that was not included in the divine game plan. Jesus saw it for what it was and stood firm on God's Word. YOU shall not put the Lord your God to the test. Either Jesus trusted His Father or He did not.

The subtle thing here is that Satan is not denying God's faithfulness in the past which is an indisputable fact. But what He has done is tried to ignore it by focusing doubt on the current moment. He wants you to be asking what God has done for you today. Yes, we know God was faithful in the past, but is that any guarantee for today? The past faithfulness of God in our lives has to be remembered and become an immovable anchor for our faith. It is no accident that the words "remember," "remembrance," "memorial," etc., are used over 200 times in the Bible. Why? Sinners appear to have short and often very selective memories.

Temptation #3—The temptation to rule and receive the glory of all the kingdoms of the world—and bypass the cross.

Of all the temptations, it would seem that this would be the strongest. The devil is offering Jesus all the glory and power of all the kingdoms of the earth. Sounds like a great deal. But it was all an illusion. God would eventually judge the devil and take away his power and authority. He is headed for Hell along with all those who follow him. Jesus saw through that quickly.

The real temptation was the offer to bypass the cross. According to Satan, Jesus could be the ruler of all the kingdoms of the earth and avoid all the pain, suffering, and death He was going to have to endure if He pursued the path He was on. Satan wanted Jesus to imagine all the influence for good that He could have as ruler over all mankind! But if He chose that path, there would be no way for us to be saved from the penalty of our sins. The whole thing was a lie.

Mankind does not need an influence for good, they need a Savior or they will all end up with the devil in Hell. The Scripture is clear—"...all our righteousnesses are like filthy rags..." (Isaiah 64:6 KJV). We are permanently damaged goods; we do not need reformation, we need re-creation. This was the goal of the Father; this was why He sent the Son. To accomplish the will and desire of His Father, there was only one path for Jesus: the cross. Jesus lived to worship and serve His Father alone. Therefore, in the strongest terms, He refused Satan's offer.

Again, it is crucial that we understand that Jesus defeated the devil simply by trusting God and standing on His Word. As long as He lived His life in submission to His Father, doing His Father's will, the devil could have no part in His life.

As we saw earlier, virtually the whole book of Deuteronomy can be summed up in the phrase, "Beware, lest you forget." Sadly, Israel was not able to grasp this. They paid (and continue to pay) a steep price in their sufferings. We do not want to make the same mistake.

How is the Devil Likely to Try to Tempt Us?

The list of ways may actually be endless, but here are a few examples (some of them may sound familiar!). For some reason I cannot explain, a lot of them tend to be "D" words.

Doubt: The major goal of any temptation.
- "Has God said _____?" You fill in the blank.
- "Did God really mean _____? Does Scripture really say that? Isn't that extreme?"
- "IF you are the Son of God, do this —."
- "Sure, God has been faithful up to now, but look at the things you have done. Will He still be faithful to you? You know you do not deserve it."

Disappointment:
- "You have been so faithful to God, why wouldn't He answer this prayer the way you wanted?"
- "What good does it do to trust God, you never get what you ask for?"
- "You have prayed so long for_____, but nothing changes. It may even be worse now."

Disillusionment/Discouragement:
- "You must not be in the will of God. This ministry is fruitless, it is a waste of time."
- "You have labored so long and so hard, why does God not give any fruit? There must be sin in your life."
- "You have grieved the Spirit. You may have committed the unpardonable sin!"

• "You messed up again like you always do. You cannot do anything right. You are a failure."

Do these sound familiar? We could go on and on. But the reality is that God's voice is *not* the voice of condemnation. He may, indeed He will, at times rebuke us and discipline us, but it will be like that of a Father training his son. If done properly, that kind of discipline does not carry the harsh tone of condemnation that the devil uses. It is done in love and with a deep desire to restore joy to the relationship.

This point is made in Scripture many times; we simply need to believe it. We already hold the ground of victory in Christ. The goal of life is not our individual success, it is the success of the team, in our case, the Church. That success is achieved by each of us fulfilling our role in God's eternal plan. How does that happen? By our determining that in our daily life, we will do the will of God whatever that means and wherever that takes us.

This also means that if we are determined to do God's will, then God assures us He will make His will clear to us. Our part is to be "ready, willing, and able." The rest is God's responsibility. We can rest assured it will be His delight to fulfill His part.

The devil's goal will be to tempt us to veer off that plan, to think that either we have a better plan or there is something in this life more valuable than to please and obey God. In our own human strength, we will undoubtedly fail. That is why God gave us the ultimate weapon: Prayer and another "helper," the Holy Spirit.

The Ultimate Weapon: "Praying Always—Praying in the Spirit"

It is said of the famous missionary Hudson Taylor, founder of the China Inland Mission (C.I.M.), "the sun never rose on China, but that Hudson Taylor was worshiping his God." Tens of millions of Chinese Christians are in heaven today because one man chose to trust God and do His will. This was the secret of the success in his ministry. He wrote one book in his life. It was called *Union and Communion*.

If any man was going to experience spiritual warfare, it was going to be the man who traveled halfway around the world to preach the gospel to a people who would refer to him and those like him as "foreign devils." Taylor understood Ephesians 6 and said, "If the Church is to go forward evangelizing in China, it must go forward on its knees." The success of C.I.M. was a living testimony to that truth. The millions of Chinese believers who are now in the kingdom of God are there because Hudson Taylor followed God's game plan.

Union and Communion perfectly expresses the idea of "praying always, and praying in the Spirit." It is because of our faith-union with Christ that we are born again and have God's Spirit dwelling within us. He is the source of all our spiritual power; He is the One who knows the mind of God and will lead us into the will of God.

But communication requires communion, and communion with the Holy Spirit requires clean, clear relationships. Sin, grieving the Spirit, causes static and makes communion difficult, if not impossible. It is tough to know what play to run next if the coach is not talking to you or if the "noise" is so loud you cannot be sure what he is saying!

To win, you have to stay in the game mentally, emotionally, physically, and spiritually! The Packers did not just plan the game plan, have a pre-game prep talk, get excited, and then go out and play the game by themselves. They were constantly talking with the coach on every play! They needed his constant instruction. This is communion. It was the key to Jesus' life as well. He was always talking to His Father. It is the key to success in every Iron-Man's life.

John Wesley once said, "Prayer changes things." Why? It brings God and all His Sovereign power into a situation. He can make it right or make it different. His purposes will not be thwarted, He will accomplish His purpose through those who are willing to do His will.

All through the gospel accounts you read of Jesus "coming aside to pray." He spent the whole night in prayer the day before He chose the twelve disciples. What was He doing? Communing with His Father, seeking His will for which men would be chosen to be among *the Twelve*.

The disciples saw the power in His life and His dependence on prayer and fellowship with the Father. They knew they needed to know more about this and urged Him, "Lord, teach us to pray." The pattern Jesus taught them was pretty simple (honor God above all else, seek first His kingdom and its coming, and do His will; in other words, keep in close communion with God and He will use you to accomplish His game plan on earth). The key is to execute consistently the plan as He directs us. This requires constant diligence. You have to maintain constant communication with the coach. You have to "stay in the game." Sin puts you on the sidelines.

The Last Night—A Missed Opportunity

Leonardo DaVinci painted a famous portrait of the last night Jesus spent with His disciples. It is called the *Last Supper*. In the Gospel of John, chapters 13-17, John records what went on during those final hours before His betrayal. Jesus gives His disciples some final instructions, and tries to encourage them ahead of time so that when the events of the next couple of days unfold, they will not be totally devastated. Much of what He said did not really make sense until much later, but His goal was to protect them and prepare them as much as possible. The next twenty-four hours would change the world.

After finishing supper in the Upper Room, Jesus led them all out to the Garden of Gethsemane. He needed to pray. He knew what was coming, probably clearer than He ever had. He needed strengthening. As God, of course, He needed nothing. But as a man, He was facing a battle that threatened to overwhelm Him. It was His darkest hour; mankind's destiny hung on His decision.

Most of us have had the experience where we were in great need of God's strengthening and it was through the prayers of others that we were sustained in the hour of trial/temptation. In these times it is both a privilege and an obligation to "stand with our brothers and sisters." This was that time for the man, Christ Jesus—and His disciples.

This is one of those stories where we see real failure on the part of the disciples. Jesus took His three closest disciples (Peter, James, and John) deep into the garden and asked them to watch and pray with Him. Do not miss this point. At the hour of greatest need, what we often need most is for other Iron-Men to stand with us in prayer before God. This is what the Good

Shepherd needed at that moment. Sadly, He found the sheep sleeping. Three times He found them sleeping! They could not stay in the game for even an hour!

Can you imagine how bad a Bowd Dowler or a Max McGee would feel if they had dropped a potential game-winning touchdown pass in an NFL championship game? It could haunt them the rest of their lives.

This is what the Lord's disciples did; they dropped the ball at the most critical moment of the game. Peter's night would get even worse! Thankfully, for these disciples, the season was not ending; for them it was just beginning. And remember what we said earlier in the book if some failure like this happens to you, and you feel like you can never be used again. These statements can anchor you in some tough times:

"The End is not the Beginning, don't confuse them."

And:

"In the Christian life, failure is not final.
God promises forgiveness."

In the Christian life you really only have <u>one</u> main goal and challenge: "You shall love the Lord your God with all your heart and with all your soul and with all your might" (Deuteronomy 6:5).

If you get this right, everything else will work out just fine. God will see to it.

We want to close with the story of a true, Iron-man Christian and the life-changing effect of his influence on others.

Chapter Twenty

A True Iron-Man Christian:
David Livingstone

"I will go anywhere, provided it be forward."
—David Livingstone

W hen the men in England who received his body and heard the story, they were astounded. Like the apostle Thomas, long ago, they refused to believe it at first. They demanded proof.

"Nine months? That is not possible! It can't be true, can it? Is it really him?"

Nobody had a clue 40 years earlier when the lion attacked and maimed him for life that the only way to identify the body of David Livingstone would be the 19th century version of an artificial joint which the doctor had put in his arm because of a lion's attack. When the lion attacked him, he marked him for life. But that was the price he had willingly paid to see the work of God succeed among the Africans. He was not going to be denied. His life was a fair price for success.

The Africans saw the difference his gospel made in a life. How? They saw its power in his life. He lived it out as he traveled all through the heart of Africa, taking the "light of the gospel" into the "dark continent." They saw his life laid down for others just like the One of whom he spoke. It was the same picture of kindness, humility, love, and grace that he preached to them. The message and the messenger were one and the same. The Spirit of the One of whom he spoke was alive in him. The impact was powerful. It won their hearts to God.

* * * * *

Now, forty years later, it was their turn to comfort and care for him. They saw him kneeling by his cot. It was about 4 am. They could see dimly into the little hut, see him on his knees before his God. They had seen it many times before. What they did not realize, and what made it different this time was, he was now absent from the body and present with His Lord in glory. He died kneeling by his bed.

This was the Iron-man, David Livingstone. Today, he is buried in Westminster Abbey. That in itself is a miracle. A miracle of love and determination and honor. You will see why.

The impact the life of Livingstone had on those who followed him was the amazing thing. So profound was the effect, so revered and precious did they esteem this life that when he died, they determined that he must be returned to his home and be buried among his people with the honor he deserved.

This might not be so remarkable under normal circumstances. But to make this decision deep in the heart of Africa in 1873 was very different. It meant that someone would literally have to carry him for nine months, over a thousand miles (!) through some of the most perilous, dangerous, and treacherous parts of Africa just to get him to the coast where he could be carried by ship to England. Led by two of his most loyal servants, that journey was accomplished. It was an awe-inspiring testimony to the love, honor, and esteem which the Africans held for him.

When his decayed body arrived later in England almost a year to the day, the only evidence that would convince many that this impossible journey was real was the artificial joint that had been used to fix his arm from the lion's bite some forty years ago.

David Livingstone wrote only one hymn during his life. The refrain of that hymn is a testament to his life.

> Lord, send me anywhere, only go with me;
> Lay any burden on me, only sustain me;
> Sever any tie,
> Save the tie that binds me to Thy heart;
> Lord Jesus, my King,
> I consecrate my life, Lord, to Thee."

While few could have penned these words with anything more than a passionate desire that they might one day become reality in their lives, Livingstone lived them.

Since that day, they have launched many a missionary's career. While the words almost seem extreme to some in this modern age, to Livingstone, it was the natural response of a true follower of Christ. His "Iron-Man" logic was summed up when he said,

"If a commission by an earthly king is considered an honor, how can a commission by a Heavenly King be considered a sacrifice?"

The logic cannot be denied. He understood what Paul meant when he said, "I am a debtor, under obligation to all men, both to Greeks and barbarians." The heathen Africans had never had the light of the gospel. These men, made in the image of God, would die and go to hell if someone did not take the gospel of Jesus Christ to them. The Lord had been clear in His commission to His disciples, "Go therefore and make disciples of all the nations" (Matthew 28:19a). His true disciples have always responded. Livingstone did as well. He had a life to give. His response to God was simple, like Isaiah before him, "Here am I, Lord, send me." The rest is history.

The world attaches little value to his labors for the gospel. But the reward of his faithfulness will be seen by all as thousands upon thousands of African saints are gathered in heaven to glorify the Lord. As the Lord looks upon them, imagine the joy Livingstone will experience when Jesus turns to him and in divine delight utters those words we all long to hear: "Well done, Livingstone."

What would your response be to His call? What is your response? He is calling.

Lombardi: "I Need Living Examples of Real Dedication."

When Vince Lombardi first got to Green Bay and looked at the game tapes of the Packers' losing 1957-58 season, he knew one thing was for certain: He had to change the whole mindset of this team. He knew exactly whom to call. He called Emlen Tunnel.

Few know his name today. In the 1950's, he was known as the Giants' "offense on defense." As a defensive back, he held the record for career interceptions for almost 20 years. He was always a tremendous athlete, but to Lombardi he was much more than that. Why?

Emlen Tunnel was the first black athlete inducted into the NFL Hall of Fame. Most people today have never even heard of him, but those who played with him were very aware of him. He was by far the best defensive back of his era. But that was not the main reason Lombardi called him. Tunnel was now in the twilight of his football career, still very good, but not the dominant player he used to be. He was even considering retiring when he got the call from Lombardi. Tunnel had something much more valuable to offer the Packers than just football skills; what Lombardi wanted most was the man himself.

Tunnel played for Vince when he coached the New York Giants. Not only was he a terrific athlete, but like Lombardi, he was a true man of character. Lombardi knew he desperately needed men of character, men who could overcome adversity, men who knew how to win. The Packers needed to have some of these men in their locker room, men with a winner's mindset.

Lombardi did not want arrogance, nor did he need oversized egos. He wanted confidence born out of experience, a winner's experience. He wanted an overcomer, a man who had faced adversity and come out victorious. He wanted men who would give all they had, all the time. He wanted an Iron-Man.

Emlen Tunnel was that kind of man.

Tunnel knew what kind of man Lombardi was, too. At the beginning, he was not sure even Vince could turn the franchise at Green Bay into a winner, but he knew Vince Lombardi. If anyone could do it, he was the man. He said of Lombardi, "You had to walk proud when you were with him." Tunnel chose to follow Lombardi to Green Bay—and became a winner, again.

Do we as followers of Christ have the same sense of honor in walking with the Lord as Emlen Tunnel did of Lombardi, that "we have to walk proud when we are with Him?" We certainly should have it. We should be echoing loudly Paul's claim, "I am not ashamed of the gospel, for it is the power of God!"

Lombardi's Legacy

Vince Lombardi was an Iron-Man. He was not just a winner on the scoreboard. He was a winner in the hearts of those who followed him, both on and off the field. He was a living example of dedication, of upright character, discipline, sacrifice, and devotion. In places where the words had never been heard before, he told his men, "You've got to have love for one another."

Lombardi knew they could not accomplish their ultimate goals simply by following him; they had to be willing to lay down their lives for one another. This is what made them the ultimate team. This made them unstoppable. This made them Iron-Men, the best of the best. Today, in honor and recognition of this legacy, the winner of the Super Bowl receives the Lombardi trophy.

Vince Lombardi took 22 men and made them into Iron-Men. He took losers and turned them into winners. For nine years they dominated the NFL.

If that legacy is worth the esteem and honor with which it is hallowed today, what is the value and worth of what Jesus Christ did? He took twelve men, mostly losers in the world's estimation, and changed the world forever. His legacy continues to change lives today.

The world is waiting to see Iron-Man Christians. If the gospel is true, they have a right to expect them. If the Packers saw enough in Vince Lombardi to follow him, believing he could make them winners, do we not see enough in Jesus Christ to believe He can make us winners, that He could use us to turn our families, our cities, our nation back to God?

He has a plan and a purpose, He just needs Iron-Men who are willing to follow His Son to victory. Will you be one? Will you follow Him?

As we began, so we will end. To paraphrase the Lord Jesus Christ:

If You Want To Win, You Must Follow Me;

There Is No Plan B.

The Bible makes it clear that the Lord is still looking for men who will follow Him. Will He find one in you? He will if your heart is completely given to Him. He will make you an Iron-Man.

The words of this hymn containing David Livingstone's prayer will surely resonate as every Iron-Man's anthem.

> O Lord, since Thou hast died
> To give Thyself for me,
> No sacrifice could be too great
> For me to make for Thee.
>
> Refrain:
> Lord, send me anywhere,
> Only go with me;
> Lay any burden on me,
> Only sustain me.
> Sever any tie, save the tie
> That binds me to Thy heart—
> Lord Jesus, my King,
> I consecrate my life, Lord, to Thee.

Iron-Man Christianity

I only have one life,
And that will soon be past;
I want my life to count for Christ,
What's done for Him will last.

I follow Thee, my Lord,
And glory in Thy cross;
I gladly leave the world behind
And count all gain as loss.

And Jesus said to them, "Truly I say to you...you who have followed Me...and everyone who has left houses or brothers or sisters or father or mother or children or farms for My name's sake, will receive many times as much, and will inherit eternal life."

—Matthew 19:28-29

Appendix

If the truths presented in this book have resonated with you, we would like to share with you a little about the place where we first learned them; and where many of those who first taught us still teach.

When the Lord called me out of professional sports into ministry, He first had to teach me how to follow Him. He led me to a small Bible school in Greenville, SC, called the Evangelical Institute. I did not know it in the beginning, but it was founded by an evangelist named Joseph Carroll, who labored alongside the man who founded the ministry of which I am now the U.S. National Director, Ambassadors for Christ.

During the two years I studied there, the timeless truths of Scripture were brought to life for me like they had never been before. The Old and New Testament survey courses gave me a biblical foundation for life principles I had never seen. But even more important, I saw these principles and truths being lived out before me in the lives of the staff and teachers. It made a life-altering impression on me. I knew it was all real. I knew that an intimate walk with our Lord was really possible. I was encouraged to go on.

If you or someone close to you is interested in more information about a school where the focus is on "training believers to live like Christ, for Christ, out of the riches of Christ, anywhere in the world", you can visit their website. Go to <www.eibibleschool.org>. There you will find the latest information on their courses, student curriculum, and conferences.

How You Can Help Us: Iron-Man Mini-Camps

First, share the book with others! Our mission and goal in publishing this book is to see men of all ages, but especially young men, challenged to follow Christ in a deeper, fuller way. In these difficult times when our young people are faced with deception and temptation on a scale rarely seen before, we want to be a positive force encouraging them and convincing them that the "path of righteousness" is not simply a wiser path, but by far the most satisfying and productive one. But it can only come through a wholehearted commitment to follow Christ and live for His glory. We trust this book will help them see that.

To aid in this effort, we are offering a four-session mini-Camp seminar focusing on the key principles presented in *Iron-Man Christianity*. If you or your church is interested in sponsoring a seminar for your youth group, men's group, Father/Son, or as an outreach event to the local community, please contact us. We would love to work with you.

We are trusting the Lord for both the "open doors" and the resources necessary to launch this ministry effectively. We would be delighted if you are interested in partnering with us or helping to sponsor an IMC mini-camp. We covet your prayers in our efforts to reach the young people of this generation. We all know there will be much spiritual opposition. Please direct any questions or correspondence to us at:

AFCI/Iron-Man Project, P.O. Box #1109, Cumming, GA 30028
Or: e-mail us at: <wfimc89@yahoo.com>
Or: online at: www.wfimc89.com